MARYLAND, *my* MARYLAND

Maryland, my Maryland

The Cultural Cleansing of a Small Southern State

Joyce Bennett

Maryland, My Maryland: The Cultural Cleansing of a Small Southern State

Copyright © 2016 by Joyce Bennett

ALL RIGHTS RESERVED. No part of this publication may be reproduced, distributed, or transmitted in any form or by any means, including photocopying, recording, or other electronic or mechanical methods, or by any information storage and retrieval system without the prior written permission of the publisher, except in the case of very brief quotations embodied in critical reviews and certain other non-commercial uses permitted by copyright law.

Produced in the Republic of South Carolina by

SHOTWELL PUBLISHING LLC
Post Office Box 2592
Columbia, So. Carolina 29202

www.ShotwellPublishing.com

This book was originally published by the author under the title *Letters From the Outpost: Essays on the Cultural Cleansing of a Small Southern State* (August 2014).

Cover adapted from *View of Baltimore* by William Henry Bartlett (1809-1854) by Boo Jackson TCB Designs.

ISBN-13: 978-0692722398
ISBN-10: 0692722394

10 9 8 7 6 5 4 3 2 1

For McKenzie, Carly, Hayden
and
the Maryland Division
of the
Sons of Confederate Veterans

ACKNOWLEDGEMENTS

Far from a disquisition, this book is merely a collection of essays, three of which previously appeared in *Chronicles: A Magazine of American Culture*, published by the Rockford Institute in Rockford, Illinois. Many are based on themes developed in Dispatches from Little Dixie, an occasional column I wrote a few years back for *St. Mary's Today*, a gritty, politically incorrect country weekly that printed all points of view and stood up to power. I wish to thank *SMT* publisher and editor Kenneth Rossignol, now publisher of *The Chesapeake Today*, for giving me one of my earliest opportunities to challenge popular misconceptions regarding the Old Line State.

For their assistance and encouragement, I am also indebted to Patricia Gray, Linda Reno, J. B. Couch, Jim Dunbar, Carolyn Billups, Rob Long, Jonathan Beasley and Patricia Buck, former president of the Point Lookout POW Descendants Organization. I am especially thankful to Rose Marks and Robert Marks—God grant him eternal repose—for calling my attention to so many sources of information on Maryland and the War of Secession.

And I extend my gratitude as well to Lorraine White of the Highland County (Virginia) Historical Society, Rev. David Whitney of the Institute on the Constitution and the staff of the St. Mary's County (Maryland) Historical Society. Furthermore, I wish to recognize Dr. Michael Crawford, Joe Gordon and Heidi Lenzini of the Navy History and Heritage Command for providing information on Commodore Isaac Mayo.

Finally, I thank Paul Bennett, Elizabeth Ann Bennett Mueller and my son, William Bennett Wynkoop, and daughter-in-law, Julie Wood Wynkoop, for their unfailing devotion and love.

JB

A liking sprang up for our style of dress, and the toga became fashionable. Step by step they were led to things that dispose to vice, the lounge, the bath, the elegant banquet. All this in their ignorance, they called civilization, when it was but part of their servitude.
—Tacitus

A people cannot live under condemnation and upon the philosophy of their conquerors. Either they must ultimately come to scorn the condemnation and the philosophy of those who thrust these things upon them, or their soul should and will perish.
—Frank Lawrence Owsley, in *I'll Take My Stand*

*Better the blade, the shot, the bowl,
Than crucifixion of the Soul....
Huzza! she spurns the Northern scum!*
—Lines from the Maryland State Song

CONTENTS

PRELUDE (1)

GEOGRAPHY (5)
Shrinking the South
Changes in Latitude: More on Southern Geography

A HISTORY UNRECONSTRUCTED (11)
Maryland State Song Under Attack—Again and Again
My Hometown: A Rank Secession Hole
Maryland's Revised History: A Tangled Web
Maryland History by the Numbers
The 1860 Presidential Election in Maryland
Trail of Lies
Onderdonkian History
Barbara Fritchie and Stonewall

THE SOUTHERN PERSPECTIVE ON MARYLAND (41)
Introduction
Mary Chestnut
Robert E. Lee and the Liberation of Maryland
The Angel of Chimborazo

MARYLANDERS IN THE WAR (53)
Governor Hicks: Accidental Defender of Maryland History
What Dr. Mudd Saw
Confederate Rose
Lamb to the Slaughter?
Who Was John Wilkes Booth?

MARYLAND: HEART AND SOUL OF THE CONFEDERATE NAVY (71)
Admiral Semmes: Southern Born, Southern Bred
Admiral Franklin Buchanan: Reluctant Confederate?
The Marylander on the Hunley
Isaac Mayo Unreconstructed

MORE ON HISTORY (89)

Lloyd Tilghman and the War in the West
A Distant Defender of the Old Line State
The Maryland SCV: Keeping Watch

CULTURE AND SOCIETY (95)

Growing Old in the South
Two Murders
Yankeefying Dixie
Redneck Girls and Southern Belles
Beware That Which You Don't Understand
The Country Girl
On Courtesy
The Fall of the House of Chaptico
Maryland in the Movies
Give Me That Old-Time Religion
The Devil Went Down to Dixie
I'm OK, You're...a Yankee
Saving Maryland's Southern Speech
Old Versus New Baltimore
Halfbacks and Wannabes
Name of God...Yankee Ham Hocks!
The Southerner's Love Affair with the Tomato
Maryland Cookin'
Pickin' Crabs
Hee Haw Redux
Maryland Is Hunt Country

GLOSSARY OF MARYLANDISMS (161)

NOTES (185)

PRELUDE

Country music star Miranda Lambert a few summers ago stirred up a hornet's nest when she told a crowd in Calvert County, Maryland that back home in the Lone Star State they refer to Marylanders as Yankees. After someone on stage quietly explained to her that she had committed a faux pas, Lambert, in an attenuated Texas accent, tried to placate her obviously irritated fans with the acknowledgement that Maryland is below, not above, the Mason-Dixon Line. Further into the concert, her earlier misstep apparently forgotten, she quipped that her father was of the opinion that all the pretty women come from the South, but she would have to admit Daddy was wrong because there were some nice-looking ladies in the audience. The real and more egregious insult inherent in this inapt comment was not that she had implied that Northern women are less attractive than Southern women but that for the second time, if only through insinuation, she had called fellow Southerners the "Y word." Having had enough of the cowgirl's gaucherie, the twice-offended rednecked throng began to boo and to protest that Lambert was, *by God,* in the South. Every now and then real Marylanders speak up in defense of who they are. The outraged concert goers, perhaps in spite of themselves, were taking a stand for their history, their geography and what is left of the culture of their corner of the South, not the South of the San Saba or the North Fork but that of the Potomac and the James, the South of the Carrolls and the Calverts, the Randolphs and the Lees. What has happened—is happening—in Maryland is significant because the cultural cleansing of the Old Line State partakes of the universal onslaught against all ancient and venerable civilized orders.

 Established in 1634, Maryland played a vital role in the shaping of the American republic, her conquest by the North in 1861 prefiguring the dangerous statist inclinations of the central government in the century and a half to follow. Once a well-loved daughter of the South, once renowned for her superb cuisine, fine sipping whiskey, blooded horses and air-cured tobacco, Maryland has succumbed to a Yankee consumerist culture, her centuries-old Anglo-Celtic-Southern traditions now all but lost—or seemingly so. Considered today a grimy little Northern state, her old Southern speech has been ridiculed to near extinction; her comity and graciousness have given way to Northern abruptness and vulgarity, and her history has been rewritten or forgotten.

That Maryland has been culturally cleansed is irrefutable. That her image is different now than it was just a few decades ago is easily documented. What is difficult is proving why there has been a deliberate redefining of the state from Southern to Northern and, more difficult still, proving that anyone should care that such a redefinition has taken place.

A formerly reconstructed Marylander, I came to realize during a decade-long sojourn in the Midwest what a beautiful culture I had left behind and how foolish I had been ever to have repudiated it. In the early 1980s, I returned to my home seeking the things I had once renounced, and I now speak I believe with some authority to my own erstwhile deracination, the deracination of my fellow Marylanders and the attendant pathologies and shame.

I expect that those who hold to the belief that the truth cannot be told with passion, should be told with insipid language, will dismiss what I write here because of "bias." And my words will anger many. If I were to say that Massachusetts is a Southern state, people would likely pity and even humor me thinking to themselves, "Poor thing, she ain't right." Yet I have wondered why it is that over the years my defense of Maryland's Southernness has been met not with sympathy or amused tolerance but with contention, even rage at times. A man who said he was "from Alabama"—likely a carpetbagger living there—once suggested to me that if an "in-depth analysis" is required to prove Maryland Southern then probably it is not. But I know of no other way to answer the enormity of the lies told by the subverters of culture. I am not straining to prove that Maryland is in the South; I am strenuously disproving what the liars are saying about her. Still, I know that the prejudices towards my state are almost impenetrable, the self-assurance of the unread pronouncers of things Southern and Northern unshakable.

And I admit to being discouraged not so much by the outsiders and intruders who re-enforce the lies but by kinsmen and old friends who have denied their birthright out of ignorance, apathy or fear. I am not without at least some hope, however, that Maryland, or some of her counties, can yet know a renaissance. In the meantime, leaving to others the full explication of the effects of the reconstruction of history and culture, I only wish to bear witness to what Jefferson Davis knew so long ago, that "the story of Maryland is sad to the last degree."[1]

GEOGRAPHY

Shrinking the South

Having culturally cleansed Maryland and her sister states in the Upper South, Northerners are proceeding to change other areas of the Southland at an alarming rate. Enveloped in an intellectual fog, some of these newcomers to Dixie, when they can get away with it, even deny that they are living in the South.

Attracted to rural and urban Southern communities alike because of their peace and charm and the employment opportunities they provide for overly credentialed and undereducated snow birds, relocating Yankees irrationally seek to destroy the very things that bring them to the South in the first place. Their high-end carpetbags hardly unpacked, they begin to muscle in on county boards and historical societies to "make a difference" and to bring about "progress." In January of 2007, a friend of mine was shopping in Richmond and was told by a sales clerk, a transplanted New Yorker, that the multitudes of Northerners who had been moving to Virginia had improved the Old Dominion. Living in Yankee conclaves in the former capital of the Confederacy and avoided by polite Richmond society, they actually believe they are saving a benighted and backward people.

Though carpetbaggers have been "improving" Maryland for some time now, in spite of their best efforts, there remain the stubborn vestigial remnants of this small Southern state's culture kept alive by the inconsiderate, intractable few of us who refuse to speak and act Northern. But those who seek to destroy our Southernness are relentless even when confronted with historical truths or Maryland's very geography.

As far back as the 1860 presidential election there were those who wanted to redefine the Old Line State to their own ends. The *New York Tribune* confidently predicted that Lincoln would win Maryland[1]—he received only two and a half percent of the popular vote. And as the war began, the *New York World* declared that Maryland's "material interests" were those of the North but warned that the desires of the people of Maryland did not matter and that conquest and occupation could easily be the fate of their state.[2] The truth is that Northerners at that time more typically viewed Maryland as an impudent Southern province to be occupied and subjugated, and in 1865, texts such as *Mitchell's Primary Geography*, published in Philadelphia, still included it in the South.[3]

But by the 1890s, the *Confederate Veteran* found it necessary to defend Maryland insisting that it was "emphatically a Southern State, notwithstanding it had come to be classed with...the Middle States."[4] Nevertheless, as late as the 1970s, Maryland was generally considered part of the Southland. This region is not, however, all alligators and palm trees, and the weather of the Upper South can be bitter in the winter. In February 1862, from Camp Allegheny in the highlands of the Old Dominion, a young lieutenant named Shepherd Green Pryor wrote to his wife, Penelope, complaining about snow-filled entrenchments and expressing his regiment's regrets that they were "a long way" from their "warm homes in Sumter Co., Georgia."[5]

In spite of cold mountains, today Virginia's geography is not as much a target of revisionism as is Maryland's. Though TV weather reporters occasionally include Virginia in the Northeast, sometimes (along with North Carolina) in a new and ever-expanding Mid-Atlantic region, most often they generously "allow" Virginia its Southern location. On the other hand, they "move" Maryland in and out of the Mid-Atlantic but usually isolate it from Virginia "placing" it in the North, an absurd geographical reclassification. Many summer evenings, I have waited anxiously for storms that have already pounded Northern Virginia to move south into Southern Maryland where I live. Virginia's weather is Maryland's.

A poor grasp of real Southern geography can be a disadvantage. A contestant appearing on *Who Wants to Be a Millionaire*, reaching the

$125,000 level, only four questions away from winning one million dollars, answered "Virginia and Maryland" when he was asked which two states are separated by the Mason-Dixon Line. He lost all but $32,000 of his previous winnings.

Those who believe Maryland is in ice-bound New England while just to its east lie Virginia and the sunny South will probably be surprised to learn that Maryland ranks number three in the frequency of occurrence of twisters,[6] phenomena associated with the South and the Midwest. Maryland definitely does not fall into the latter category. Those Old Line State natives who can still predict weather by observing the direction of a morning breeze or the suppleness of a hand of tobacco in high order know that it is anything but a rare event when a waterspout snakes across a river or a whirlwind touches down in field or forest. It is true that our state is looking increasingly Yankee as more Northern-style McMansions are built here, and more farmers are painting our graying tobacco barns Old MacDonald red, but our weather doesn't lie. Tornadoes and hurricanes blow here. Cypress and magnolias, peanuts and cotton can be found growing here at a latitude that remains Southern and a constant in a relativistic world.

Changes in Latitude: More on Southern Geography

From the rough stormy Atlantic washing the shores of many distant lands, one passes into the comparatively smoother waters of the Chesapeake Bay, shut in by the friendly arms of Maryland and Virginia. —Charles Lee Lewis, *Admiral Franklin Buchanan: Fearless Man of Action*

Just as there will always be an England (though it is no longer free), the South will endure. But where is it? An old dictionary of mine defines it as "that part of the United States south of Mason and Dixon's line, the Ohio River, and...Missouri and Kansas." This runs contrary to the popular notion

Joyce Bennett

that the Potomac divides North from South. As beautiful as this river is, it is not a valid delineation of the two regions since it flows an anfractuose southeasterly course from its headwaters in the Virginia Highlands to its broad confluence with the Chesapeake Bay. There is as much a north-south component to it as there is an east-west one. Western Charles County, Maryland and Mason's Neck, Virginia, for example, are both north and south of the Potomac. I contend that the South commences at the boundary between Pennsylvania and Maryland, but because perception is geographical reality these days, many will argue that the Mason-Dixon is "descending."

Even Southerners—especially Southerners—disagree on the definition of the South. Some consider Missouri and West Virginia Southern states; others don't. And while the NRA classifies Maryland as Southern, as do a few heritage organizations, generally speaking this designation is now rarely applied to Virginia's neighbor. That Maryland has been reconstructed pleases the state's native Northerner-wannabes and their masters, the Yankee transplants who instruct our children not to say *y'all* and who are trying to outlaw the Maryland State Song because of its offensive "Southern" lyrics.

An acquaintance of mine believes that because the North is making inroads in the upper reaches of Dixie, the South now begins at Richmond. If that logic is followed, then the "line," given that Virginia's culture is threatened and the fact that the Tar Heel State is under "invasion," will soon be located at the northern border of South Carolina— but not for long as the restless Yankee is always looking farther southward. And urban, aging gays who have grown tired of "fashionable" Washington D.C. and Fredericksburg, Virginia are now busy buying up retirement "property" in Charleston. Attracted to its architecture and "waterfront" and to its graciousness, a quality once possessed by the two aforementioned towns (D.C.'s charm admittedly having died many decades ago), they will soon grow tired of the graciousness because they love Charleston only for its bones not for its Southern soul.

What is at work in Maryland, Virginia and the Carolinas is also Alabamy bound. One Friday a Yankee now living in that Deep South state called in to neoconservative Chris Plante's Washington, D.C. radio talk show and commented that lots of people from Ohio and New England are carpetbagging to the Heart of Dixie. He extended an invitation to "come on down" to Plante's listening audience, mainly composed of expatriate New Yorkers, Pennsylvanians and sundry Northerners now calling themselves Marylanders and Virginians. Will the Mason-Dixon "fall" below Alabama if Yankees ruin it? And how does a very culturally-cleansed Florida fit into this new way of looking at geography?

Of course it is illogical to allow cultural integrity to determine the actual location of the South. But logic is lost on most people today, including those Southern people who might grudgingly admit that Maryland is in the South but who really down deep think even blooded Marylanders are Yankees, to us an inaccurate and galling label. No matter how many times we object to the characterization and explain why, they politely listen, then soon forget and revert to thinking our state is above the Mason-Dixon, actually, "north of the Potomac," a question-begging epithet as I've said.

And no one it seems looks at maps anymore, or, if they do, they fail to read them correctly. One of the problems with map reading is maps. Because the flat plane projection of a global Earth necessitates the distortion—on paper—of latitude and longitude, maps that more faithfully depict longitude at the expense of latitude leave the impression that Maryland is much farther north than it is. Maps that sacrifice longitude to latitude manifest the Old Line State's actual location and clearly demonstrate that what there is of Maryland lies east of West Virginia and Virginia. For a little more geographical perspective, Annapolis is south of the cities of Leesburg and Winchester, Virginia, and Maryland's southernmost point is well south of Charlottesville.

Still, the average person will say that Kentucky is way down yonder near Louisiana and that Maryland is somewhere up around Maine. But the Old Line State begins and ends in the South. Latitude forces the final judgment: Conquered and disgraced as it is, its capital city held by carpetbaggers, Maryland has been Southern since 1634. The South is at once a recognized cultural entity while composed of disparate elements: Celtic, Saxon, French,

African, Spanish. These elements have added to and shaped that primordial Southland formed by Virginia and Maryland, sister states whose Tidewater culture was the *fons et origo* of what we call Dixie today.

A HISTORY UNRECONSTRUCTED

*Natura inest in mentibus nostris insatiabilis
quaedam cupiditas veri videndi.*—Cicero

Maryland State Song Under Attack—Again and Again

Drive down a deserted street, and it is easy to forget what has become of Maryland's capital. But my visit there on a Wednesday in 2009 to attend a House of Delegates committee hearing brought home to me with depressing clarity that this small, still-picturesque city crawling now as it is with drab and determined carpetbaggers is the seat of power for those who hate Maryland's Southern heritage and history. Annapolis has become a battleground where cultural cleansers in the General Assembly, pressured by the *nouveaux venus* they represent, continue to mount an assault on the most despised symbol of that heritage, that history, the Maryland State Song.

With the introduction in 2001 of House Bill 1057, Delegate Peter Franchot, a native of Connecticut, unsuccessfully sought to repeal James Ryder Randall's "controversial" lyrics; about a year later in the Maryland Senate, the sponsors of SB 19 failed in their attempt to replace them with those of poet John T. White.

> *Proud sons and daughters boast of thee,*
>   *Maryland, My Maryland.*
> *Thine is a precious history,*
>   *Maryland, My Maryland.*
> *Brave hearts have held they honor dear,*
> *Have met the foeman far and near,*
> *But victory has furnished cheer,*
>   *Maryland, My Maryland.*

White's 1894 poem, flowery and effeminate, denies the very "precious history" to which it alludes.

Joyce Bennett

In his fiery verses, Randall recalls the bravery of the Maryland Line during the Revolutionary War, as he urges his people to join Virginia and to rise up against the tyranny of the North, to fight on behalf of Baltimore citizens killed by Yankee troops in April 1861. Resentful that their now-Northern, now-Utopian Maryland is still haunted by history, carpetbaggers find most unsettling the words contained in these stanzas of Randall's poem.

> *The despot's heel is on thy shore,*
> > *Maryland!*
> *His torch is at thy temple door,*
> > *Maryland!*
> *Avenge the patriotic gore*
> *That flecked the streets of Baltimore,*
> *And be the battle queen of yore,*
> > *Maryland! My Maryland!*
>
> *Thou wilt not yield the Vandal toll,*
> > *Maryland!*
> *Thou wilt not crook to his control,*
> > *Maryland!*
> *Better the fire upon thee roll,*
> *Better the blade, the shot, the bowl,*
> *Than crucifixion of the soul,*
> > *Maryland! My Maryland!*
>
> *I hear the distant thunder-hum,*
> > *Maryland!*
> *The Old Line's bugle, fife, and drum,*
> > *Maryland!*
> *She is not dead, nor deaf, nor dumb—*
> *Huzza! she spurns the Northern scum!*
> *She breathes! she burns! she'll come! she'll come!*
> > *Maryland! My Maryland!*

Maryland, My Maryland

Randall's poetry is an embarrassment to those desperately trying to divert attention from Maryland's "odious" Southern-fried past.

In 1960 Maryland's Governor Tawes "issued a proclamation" designating the first week in 1961 as James Ryder Randall Week. The *Evening Star's* Anne Christmas never once uses the term *controversial* in her December 31, 1960 article on the governor's honoring of Randall and the song, providing a concise, straightforward and factual account of the history of the "Marseillaise of the Confederate cause."[1] But, echoing many in the media elite today, *Washington Post* staff writer Lori Montgomery, obviously discomfited by Maryland's creepy history, in a March 2001 article, puzzles that "for reasons that remain a mystery" the General Assembly adopted "Maryland! My Maryland!" as the state song in 1939.[2] Noting that "the last time a state lawmaker tried to tamper with 'Maryland, My Maryland,' his office received death threats," Montgomery nevertheless assumes a Northern identity for Maryland and finds the "debate" over the state's "lurid Confederate" anthem "surprisingly passionate." To resolve the tension between the truth about Maryland and accepted revisionist lies, she employs the non sequitur: Maryland "remained loyal to the Union but only after Lincoln imprisoned a good portion of the General Assembly to head off a secession vote." To support further her Maryland-as-Yankee-state premise Montgomery quotes former state senator Howard A. Denis: "Maryland is not just the Maryland we see in the Washington suburbs....In Southern Maryland and the Eastern Shore, slavery was the underpinning of the economy. Out there, Lincoln didn't get too many votes." Denis's "history lesson" goes unchallenged by Montgomery who allows it to imply that Lincoln triumphed elsewhere in Maryland. He didn't. He failed miserably all over the state. But left-wing journalists like Montgomery either don't know or won't acknowledge this.

Not to be outdone in rewriting the past, the sponsors of SB 19 and HR 1057 justified their proposed repeal of James Ryder Randall's words with the contention that Randall wrote his poem to "articulate his Confederate sympathies." This suggests that Randall wasn't a Southerner but merely had Southern sentiments. But Randall was a Southerner who had left his Maryland for a sister state in the deeper South. His taking a teaching position there was not unusual because in the mid-nineteenth century strong ties still existed between Maryland and Louisiana, both centers of Southern Catholicism, Marylanders often moving to Louisiana and Louisianans to Maryland. Pointe Coupee Parish had not made a separatist out of Randall; he had not learned to love secession there—resistance to tyranny was in his Southern blood.

Now the Maryland state comptroller, Peter Franchot, when he served in the House of Delegates, began his attack on Maryland's martial hymn at the urging of a Montgomery County student. Ben Meiselman complained, "The words are dense and hard to understand. And, basically, they tell Maryland to secede from the Union....Most parts you can't understand. And the parts I can understand, I don't like."[3] Concerning the campaign conducted by this boy and his father to rid Maryland of her problematic Southernness, the late columnist Sam Francis called on native Marylanders to stand up for their state song and for all that it means.

> *It's not surprising that in the First Universal Nation being manufactured in Washington, Hollywood, and New York, such values have to go, the events that embody them have to be forgotten and any song that enshrines them in its lyrics can't be sung. If Marylanders were really still Marylanders, they'd sing their state song more often and louder than ever—and politely suggest to the Meiselman family that it might be happier if it moved to Massachusetts.*[4]

But these First Universal Nationalist types, these Yankees, just won't go home.

And they made another move against "Maryland! My Maryland!" in 2009 introducing House Bill 1241. The Northerners and scalawags who now prevail on most issues in the chambers of the State House are particularly incensed by the line "Huzza! she spurns the Northern scum!" At the Health and Government Operations Committee hearing on the bill, the hearing I attended, its proponents resorted to the usual recitation of suspect statistics, insisting that the Maryland song be revised because more "Marylanders" fought for the North than the South. The number of those from the Old Line State who wore blue is greatly inflated and varies depending on which revisionist is speaking. The truth is that no one knows exactly how many Marylanders fought for the Yankees, but there were most likely fewer of them than those who went to the aid of the Confederacy (see "Maryland History by the Numbers").

Also at the hearing that day were the supporters of HR 1178, a bill that proposed a special version of the Maryland state song "singable for school children." Four young ones carefully selected to represent the correct ethnicities stood before the committee to speak in favor of this new "child-friendly" song and in opposition to the current song. After these four gave their testimony, they joined their fellow classmates in singing in sweetly off-key voices the children's lyrics written by the late Tom Wisner. Just as easily applied to any of the tempest tossed who have washed up on America's shores at various times, this generic doggerel tells the story of the crossing of the Atlantic by the original settlers of Lord Baltimore's colony.

The children receiving enthusiastic applause, momentum seemed to be swinging in the direction of the revisionists in the room. And the defenders of history alone received tough questions from the committee—at least from those committee members who weren't playing solitaire on their laptops or chatting or jumping up to leave the room from time to time. One delegate asked an anti-HR 1241 speaker if there had been any "students of color" (which means colored students) in his 1950s elementary school class. This was a debating trick clearly intended to divert attention from the real issue: Should Maryland's state song be changed to advance the larger objective of finishing the job of reconstructing Maryland, to make the state more "respectably" Northern and therefore more to the liking of an increasingly "diverse," South-despising population?

The Northerners who have relocated to Maryland and who want it to be Rhode Island seem to begrudge us even the smallest token of our culture. On the way to the hearing, I noticed a memorial to the late Louis

L. Goldstein, Maryland comptroller for many years. Inscribed on his monument is "God bless you all real good," the more Northern version of his signature slogan "God bless y'all real good"—the *real good* not the *y'all*, in this instance, taking the grammatical liberties. Although he spoke with an "old-time" Calvert County, Maryland accent, his Southern charm was only superficial, and this Pappy O'Daniel in my opinion did not deserve a statue in Annapolis. As he is remembered with one, however, the words ascribed to him on that memorial should be his.

With all of the frenzied attacks on Maryland's culture, "Maryland! My Maryland!" miraculously remains intact. Though short-haired Yankee women, Connecticut metrosexuals and carpetbagger brats "from" Montgomery County will keep agitating for our cultural demise—and may eventually win the "song wars"—the unreconstructed will not crook to their control or dance to a Yankee tune.

My Hometown: A Rank Secession Hole

One evening in 1910, a man who worked for the *Baltimore Sun* checked in to Hotel St. Mary's in Leonardtown, Maryland. Apologizing that he couldn't promise a very good meal because it was "long past the supper hour," the "landlord" served him an improvised feast of "soft crabs done to a turn, a shad roe, Maryland biscuits, hot cornbread, a salad and coffee."[1] The reporter took up residence at the hotel for a time writing a series of dispatches extolling the generosity and warmth of the people of Leonardtown and surrounding St. Mary's County. A few years earlier, another visiting correspondent, though disappointed by what he considered the town's less-than-"picturesque" appearance, had praise for the "delicate politeness," hospitality and gentle Southern speech of the local citizens.[2] Today, Southern hospitality and accents are in short supply at the new Executive Inn located not far from where Hotel St. Mary's stood before it burned to the ground many decades ago. And guests at the former will eat bagels not biscuits at their complimentary continental breakfast. As Yankeefied as it has become, Leonardtown, like it or not, has a Southern history.

In the 1950s it was a segregated place. But at the Joyce Ann Shop, the pretty proprietress, my mother, who sold stylish dresses at "discount" prices, would welcome those who stood in her doorway inquiring if she "served colored." A family friend remembers buying from Mama the outfits and hats she wore to local celebrations held on the fifteenth of *Oh gust* (August), a holy day of obligation but in the fifties also a festive occasion for those of African descent in our community. Mama's black patrons, however, understood that they could not ask to try on those holiday dresses. They knew also that they were expected to sit in the balcony at the New Theater and upstairs at St. Aloysius Church, that they could not go to the same restaurants as whites did, that their children—until 1965—could not attend the same public schools. And when my father carried Agnes, our housekeeper-baby sitter, from her home to ours, she sat in the back seat of the family car because the conventions about who sat where in automobiles at that time were strictly observed.

Agnes, who did not know how old she was and who called my baby brother Paul Oyster Cake, would watch American Bandstand and dance while she ironed clothes—I still remember the aroma o f steam-pressed cotton on hot afternoons and Agnes in a blue maid's uniform moving to the beat behind the ironing board. And Agnes would entertain us with tales of her Saturday night adventures down "The Alley," the popular name for the west end of Leonardtown's Park Avenue which ran along one side of the corner Rexall. A sort of social center where chain smokers played the slots, and teenagers drank cherry cokes at the snack bar in the back, the Rexall was well stocked with paper dolls, candy cigarettes and other 1950s childhood treasures.

Park Avenue terminated about half a city block away from the drug store and was off limits to whites other than health department officials and the sheriff. The Alley was notorious for taverns like Fat Man Charley's, Sis's Hide-A-Way and a spot Agnes called the beer garden, where one evening she spied a woman wearing my mother's new crinoline. The woman, who worked for my parents occasionally when Agnes needed a day off, had stolen it, and, as the thief twirled to the shake, rattle and roll of the music, Agnes caught a glimpse of the red netting of the crinoline under her full skirt. Right there on the dance floor she took it off of her. My mother was touched by this display of loyalty and loved Agnes for it.

My father also had great affection for Agnes, despite the fact that he held views on race that would be unpopular these days. The same year I was born, Daddy had built our house in the midst of black neighbors whom he liked and respected, and yet, he sharply chastised my sister and me one time for having made mud pies next door with two little girls about our age. I was confused by my father's proscription and felt that there was something not quite right about what he said. But I was nonetheless very much a product of a culture that separated the races.

The Joyce Ann Shop was located in a nineteenth-century building that looked out on a memorial to the World War I dead, the white soldiers' names engraved on bronze plaques on one side of it, the names of the "colored" on the other. It never occurred to me when I was coming along that this was in any way remarkable. The monument is still there, but a few years back, a "local" newspaper, the *Enterprise*, a subsidiary (at least at the time) of the *Washington Post*, called for the removal of the plaques suggesting that they could be given to the Historical Society and that the *Enterprise* was not trying to "rewrite" history. In spite of attempts by "journalists" to alter that which is in reality unalterable, at the time of this writing the memorial has not been defaced, and so it continues to tell the truth about the past.

Leonardtown's history is also embodied in Tudor Hall. Surviving today as a brick mansion with a colonnaded, recessed portico, it was once home to the Barnes family and about two hundred souls held in bondage. Richard Barnes, who died in 1804, instructed in his will that his slaves were to be emancipated though not all of them gained their freedom as state laws frustrated his intentions. [3] Built on a highpoint above Breton Bay, the house was also owned by Philip Key, kinsman to Francis Scott Key and a descendant, it is said, of England's King Henry VII.[4] One of Tudor Hall's twentieth-century residents was Colonel Swann, described as "a southern gentleman of the old school."[5] In the 1930s dressed in "summer white" and a "large southern type hat," he would hobble on his cane down the hill to meet the steamboats. Another local dignitary, Judge Camalier, was known to receive disembarking passengers at the landing as well. When the steamboat era ended, he began greeting people as they stepped off buses at Duke's Corner until the 1940s when the Navy base opened, and the newcomers sent him home in tears with their ridicule.

Though it aspires to be "upscale," and it isn't as Southern friendly as it was, there is a little of the South left in Leonardtown. There are still magnolias on the courthouse lawn and pickup trucks parked in front of the bank. And the Sons of Confederate Veterans continue to march on Veterans Day—to appreciative onlookers according to J. B. Couch of the Vincent Camalier Camp.

> *On Wednesday at the parade, we were all in Confederate uniforms and flying Confederate flags. One of our SCV members, who plays the bagpipes, marched with us, playing songs like The Bonnie Blue Flag, Amazing Grace, and Dixie....The parade spectators loved us. As we marched by they would stand, salute the Confederate flags, and applaud. I threw doubloons (like the ones they throw at Mardi gras) that had the Battle Flag on one side and the SCV logo on the other side. Kids would come into the street and beg for them.[6]*

As hard as Northern transplants have worked to "make over" Leonardtown with their Earth Day celebrations and other new age festivals, they have been unable to banish the SCV and their flags from the public square.

And even if they could, history remains. Greatly outnumbering and seldom interacting with natives, first-, second- and third-generation carpetbaggers, however, have so successfully foisted upon us what passes for their culture, they are now confused and annoyed by any evidence of our Southernness, by any evidence of that which they seemingly have destroyed.

And nothing disturbs them as much as the true story of Leonardtown in the "Civil War."

In the early days of the conflict, one Unionist newspaper called our county seat a "rank secession hole"[7] that "[bore] watching" (Ibid., August 22, 1861). When the news of Fort Sumter reached Leonardtown, church bells rang and the "wildest enthusiasm broke forth" among the citizens (Ibid., April 25, 1861), many men, according to legend, riding out to Mrs. Silence's Tavern to talk about the prospect of war with the North. Just days after the Battle of Baltimore, the citizenry resolved to raised $10,000 to arm themselves against the Yankees and to aid the seceded Southern states in securing their independence (Ibid., May 2, 1861). But by the summer of 1861, Northern troops were marching into town and in the days that followed established an encampment just to its west in an area known as Sheep-pen Woods (the iron rings on which they tethered their horses still protruding from primeval oaks as late as the 1940s).

During the occupation, the *St. Mary's Beacon* ran editorials condemning the Lincoln regime until the Northerners shut down the paper and arrested the editor. Eluding the Yankees, boys from all over Maryland hid out at Moore's Hotel waiting for an opportune moment to cross over the Potomac to join up with Virginia units. Spies and blockade runners exchanged greetings with Northern soldiers. And grieving families, under the watchful eyes of those "little men," held funerals and buried sons who had died for the South.

There is a legend that says that during the time of the occupation in Leonardtown, Yankee soldiers would have their boots repaired at a little cobbler's shop that was located on the hillside above the steamboat landing. The shop was owned by a woman who was reputedly the mistress of a kinsman of Robert E. Lee. She was, according to the legend, the mother of this black sheep's illegitimate child, a little girl. When the Yankees would visit the shop, they would shower attention on the child and pat her on the head not having any idea that she was blood kin to the great General Lee.

Maryland, My Maryland

Before the last of the Yankees had gone back north, life slowly began to return to normal, but the people never overcame completely the shame of occupation, which for our community, I believe, was at the heart of the collective inferiority complex that plagued us postbellum and into the modern age. For some, however, even under Yankee rule, there was solace to be found in raising money for Southern relief. In 1866 the *St. Mary's Gazette*, the paper that for a time replaced the *Beacon*, reported with a somewhat bitter note that a famous Confederate hero was coming to town to preside over a jousting tournament to benefit the South.

> *The renowned Col. Mosby it is bruited, will be present at the Tournament on Friday next and officiate as Chief Marshal of the day! Now, that "grim visaged war has smoothed his wrinkled front," the visit of the gallant Colonel to our county will be an acceptable event, and, as there is a strong desire among our people to see this great partizan leader, a general turn out may be anticipated (October 18, 1866).*

After war and reconstruction, Leonardtown was again to enjoy isolation for many years. Local residents went to the races at the fairgrounds; farmers met in the park to trade in horses named Stonewall Jackson and Jim Boy, and the debating society gathered to drink bourbon and to discuss the classics and the late conflict. In the twenties and thirties, the James Adams Floating Theater docked at the town wharf and put on plays and musicals for sold out audiences. Having walked several miles to Leonardtown, one little farm girl with chigger bites on her legs sold huckleberries to earn enough money for a ticket to an evening's performance.

In the years leading up to World War II, a time which marked the beginning of Leonardtown's transformation from polite Southern port to Anytown, USA, the pace of life was slow and pleasant but not unvisited by crime and even instances of brutality. It has had its share of corrupt town officials, Huey Long-style politicians and avaricious businessmen. Recognizing the failings of all and the cruelties of some of Leonardtown's people, I have no choice but to defend its history and insist that it be left alone to tell the truth.

Maryland's Revised History: A Tangled Web

Methinks the truth should live from age to age,
As 'twere retail'd to all posterity,
Even to the general all-ending day.
—*Richard III*, act 3, sc.1

Maryland's involvement in the War of Secession has not been of great interest to most historians, and, if mentioned at all, it is usually fictionalized. The rewriters of the past, who like to remind us that history is complex, will argue that if Marylanders were "divided " most were loyal to the Union or at least neutral. Given, however, that revisionism is by its very nature an absurd approach to any academic discipline, what really happened under Yankee rule in the "outpost of the South" is not lost to us but merely subsumed in the revisionism itself.

Often facts get in the way of spinning a yarn about a Maryland torn apart by warring unionist and secessionist passions. In the introduction to his pictorial history of Calvert County, Maryland, Carter T. Gray writes that Calvert during the war "became a very confused place." On the one hand, "many men in the county...fought for the Southern cause while, at the same time, the county was occupied by Union forces." [1] Though the Yankees did invade and hold Calvert County, it was never "confused" during the "Civil War," but, as a result of Carter's attempt to interject into real history the requisite (in regards to Maryland at least) brother-against-brother, neighbor-against-neighbor template, the reader might find himself bewildered when he learns that Calvert was both pro-secession and pro-secession and occupied besides.

The myth that the Old Line State was disengaged during the war, as if this were possible under the Lincoln regime, also has great appeal to those who love the idea of a "fair and balanced" Maryland, particularly those Marylanders who deny their Southern heritage. A great-aunt of mine, the granddaughter of a Confederate soldier, disliked discussing his military service—a less than heroic single hitch in the Virginia Infantry—but more willingly talked about what she was certain was the "neutral" stand her grandfather took on returning to occupied Maryland. She never admitted outright that he had likely run the Potomac River blockade and only alluded to his participation in the Confederate underground. Having spent fifty years of her life in the Northwest, where she was ridiculed for her Southern ways, my aunt bristled each time I introduced the subject. Finally, she told me with considerable pride that "Grandpapa would hide you out in the barn whether you were Confederate or Union," adding that her grandmother was always terrified he would be shot by the Yankees "for helping both Northern and Southern soldiers."

After years of trying to coax the truth from her, she had revealed it to me: My great-great-grandfather had risked the firing squad at Point Lookout by providing sanctuary to "rebels." A Yankee, especially a well-fed occupation soldier who was not in much danger of seeing combat, would not have had reason to hide out in barns in territory that was held by the Union; people in occupied Maryland harbored not Yankees but Confederates—escaped POWs or Southern soldiers who crossed the Potomac in search of food and medicine provided to them by a friendly local population. I learned many years ago from my grandmother, who wasn't as reluctant to talk about the war as her sister, that "Mr. Lincoln's men" had suspected my great-great-grandfather of "disloyal" activities and had searched his home. In the attic, they had rifled a trunk, which was eventually handed down in the family. When my mother was a child, old-fashioned dresses and pocketbooks were stored in it. She also tells me that my grandmother, a lifelong Southern Democrat, would "cut her eyes" towards the trunk when she spoke of the incident.

My grandmother's willingness to talk about the war at all was my good fortune. She and my great-aunt were from a family who, during the Yankee occupation, had developed the habit of being closed-mouthed, and they had inherited from them that tendency, my grandmother to a lesser degree. Because her many decades in the North had taught my great-aunt that the South had been on the wrong side in the war, she was more comfortable with a neutral rather than a secessionist Maryland. She had reinvented herself much as other border state Southerners have.

There are those who will argue that Maryland was neither divided nor neutral but simply loyal and Northern. Proponents of this indefensible historical perspective hate the Maryland state song and its "treasonous" words. They also despise the Confederate soldier on the courthouse lawn in Rockville, today a bastion of imported Northern liberalism; the rare and beautiful double-equestrian statue of Lee and Jackson in Yankee-infested old Baltimore City and the many other Southern memorials throughout the state. The fact that mobs, ignorant and angry, have not pulled them down is nothing short of a miracle.

Maryland History by the Numbers

Down-trodden, despised see brave Maryland lie,
The noblest of all States;
Up and to ransom her let each one try,
To hasten the plans of the Fates.
Her land is of the greatest beauty,
That e'er the eye gazed on;
Fearless she roused her to her duty,
Nor paused she 'till was done.
—N. G. Ridgely

It seems logical that any argument over the Old Line State's sympathies during the War of Secession boils down to the number of Marylanders who served North or South. But any serious student of the war and Maryland's role in it knows that it is impossible to quote with any authority a reckoning of real Marylanders who took up arms for either side.

Maryland, My Maryland

And no one has defined the problems inherent in understanding the Federals' own statistics on Marylanders in the Yankee forces as well as Wayde Chrismer in a paper prepared for the Greater Emmitsburg (Maryland) Historical Society.

> *The historian will go crazy who tries to determine with certainty how many Marylanders actually fought in the two armies. A faster way to an asylum is to try to learn where they came from. No two historians can agree upon the numbers involved. The History and Roster claims 62, 959; the OR's credit the state with 46,638. This writer's name-by-name check, eliminating all duplications, finds a figure of about 40,000 to be more likely correct.* [1]

But as Chrismer points out, determining exactly who those forty thousand were is all but impossible. What we do know is that 24 percent were foreign born.[2] Raphael Semmes in his memoirs mentions the questionable practices Yankee agents employed to induce "debased and ignorant" young Irishmen and other foreigners to fight for the Federals.[3] It is reasonable to conclude that there would be many immigrants joining the Union forces in an occupied coastal Southern state. Concerning another strategic Southern port of entry that fell to the Yankees, diarist Mary Chestnut writes, "Thousands are enlisting on the other side in New Orleans. Butler holds out inducements. To be sure, they are principally foreigners who want to escape starvation."[4]

A portion of Chrismer's forty thousand were Northerners recruited above the Mason-Dixon and designated as Marylanders by Lincoln's myrmidons[5] in an attempt to fill Maryland's quota, a quota never satisfied.[6] And even pro-Lincolnian regime historian James McPherson admits that nine thousand of the Union troops from Maryland were of African descent.[7] Although some will cry "racism" when it is suggested that black men who took up arms for the Union should not be counted in the final tally of Marylanders who served the North, the plain truth is that the fact that there were many blacks in the Yankee army in an occupied Southern state such as Maryland should come as no surprise; in an unoccupied Southern

25

state, however, there would have been no opportunity for the Union to recruit or conscript slaves or freemen. Blacks fought for the Confederacy as well, but they had no voice in the secession issue. They could not "choose sides." Their level of participation on behalf of the Southern cause is not a valid factor in determining how strong secessionism was in the unoccupied South; similarly, high numbers of black soldiers in Georgia units fighting for the North—if, hypothetically speaking, that state had been conquered early in the war— would not be a factor in determining the strength of unionism in Georgia.

Regarding the number of Maryland Confederates, out of the necessity of protecting loved ones left to the tender mercies of the occupiers, secrecy surrounded their absconding across the Potomac. And many joined Virginia or other units and were not categorized as Marylanders. Further, records are sketchy or lost. Though no historian can say with certainty how many Marylanders fought for the South, most agree that there were between twenty- and twenty-five thousand men from the Old Line State in the Confederate army. Subtracting from Wayde Chrismer's forty thousand, the total number of immigrants, Northerners and slaves and freemen—because of the reasons stated above—there were likely fewer Marylanders who wore blue than Marylanders who wore gray.

Over fifty years ago a "Civil War" Centennial Plaque was dedicated at the State House in Annapolis. Honoring "both sides" including the "nearly 63,000" Marylanders who served the Union, it's language and "moderate" sentiments, inspired by 1960s revisionism, are an offense to the truth. The plaque should be removed.

The 1860 Presidential Election in Maryland

A war has been made, at Baltimore....The violent measures which have been resorted to, have gone far to establish the fact that Maryland is retained in the Union only by military force. They have undoubtedly increased the dislike of the people to their

Maryland, My Maryland

Northern rulers. —Lord Lyons, British Minister to the
United States, in a letter to Earl Russell, September 16, 1861

Some historians point to Maryland's occupation-reconstruction voting patterns as evidence of the state's Northern "persuasion." But who would think of calling Tennessee or Louisiana Northern because Lincoln carried them in 1864? Would it make sense to ascribe to Alabama, Arkansas, Florida, North Carolina or South Carolina a Yankee mindset because Grant carried those states in 1868? Yet if the disenfranchisement of Marylanders under "Honest" Abe's regime is addressed at all, it is most often explained away as just another example of Lincoln's extraconstitutional treatment of "Northern" citizens. But if Lincoln worked mischief in New Jersey and New York, he did not find it necessary to conquer them. And they did not undergo reconstruction. Maryland rejected the Republicans at the polls in 1860 as did the rest of the South, and Maryland was again to reject the Republicans in 1868 when she was free of Yankee rule.

In 1860 Maryland's electorate proved more typically Southern than their neighbors in the Upper South, the state's electoral votes in the presidential election going to Breckinridge, the secessionist candidate, with John Bell a close second. Northern Democrat Stephen Douglas, however, won Missouri while Constitutional Unionist Bell took Virginia, Kentucky and Tennessee.

Receiving seventeen thousand votes in Missouri, which many people today consider a Southern state, Lincoln was the recipient of only a handful of votes in Maryland as was the case in Virginia and Kentucky. He won no county in the Old Line State.[1] He failed to receive a single vote in Queen Anne's or Worchester County on the Eastern Shore. Only one person, said to have been a transplanted Virginian, voted for Lincoln in St. Mary's, and to this day people know his name. According to local lore, a group of men waylaid him election night and tried to kill him.

Calvert, Howard and Prince George's each gave Lincoln one vote as well. He garnered two votes in Somerset and two in Talbot. Three people in Anne Arundel, six in Charles County voted for him. Fifty or fewer votes were cast for Lincoln in each of the following counties: Baltimore, Caroline, Dorchester, Kent and Montgomery. The Northern candidates, Lincoln and Douglas, receiving only 1,087 and 1,503 votes respectively, did very poorly in Baltimore City where Breckinridge won over Bell by a slim margin. And even in reputedly more-divided Western Maryland, Lincoln did not do well, the lion's share of votes there going to Breckinridge or Bell. In Allegany County, where Lincoln enjoyed the greatest popularity in the state, he still received only 520 votes, the "moderate" Southern candidate, Bell, defeating Douglas there 1,521 to 1,202.

Of the 92,649 votes cast in the Old Line State, Lincoln received only 2,296 and Douglas 6,080. The writers of a Northern history for Maryland, not to be deterred, will suggest, however, that Lincoln's defeat and Breckinridge's victory bear less on Maryland's true sentiments than do the results of that year's congressional races in the state, all won by unionist candidates.

But particularly at the beginning of the sectional strife many Southerners were unionists—the constitutional not the unconditional variety. Simkins and Roland, in *A History of the South*, describe this more cautious brand of unionism.

> *In the South the campaign of 1860 was fought between secessionist and unionist Democrats, with the Republican candidate standing as the great external menace for whom no Southerner could or would vote....Southern unionists....asked, "Why the hot haste, excitement, and precipitation?"*[2]

The Union Party also swept congressional races in Kentucky. In Maryland, a state in which a little less than half the black population were freemen, debates over emancipation and colonization raged, many Marylanders supporting the freeing of more slaves if deportation followed, most vehemently opposed to any Federal coercion in the matter.

Of the six candidates who won their bids for the U.S. House in Maryland in 1860, one of them, Henry May, was arrested by the Yankees in September of 1861. And four, John Crisfield, Cornelius

Maryland, My Maryland

Leary, Francis Thomas and Charles Calvert, voted against a joint Congressional resolution that called for Federal assistance to any state engaged in the "gradual abolishment of slavery, giving to such State pecuniary aid, to be used...to compensate for the inconveniences, public and private, produced by such change of system."[3] Many Marylanders were pro-slavery, but many others believed as did Henry Kyd Douglas that it was a "curse." For them, it was not the ending of slavery that presented the problem, but how it was to come about. In December of 1862, Crisfield and Calvert voted "nay" on the adoption of a resolution in support of Lincoln's Emancipation Proclamation. None of Maryland's other representatives in the House voted on the resolution (Ibid., 557n). They were treading lightly.

It is not their election of unionists to the House but their repudiation of Lincoln in 1860 that gives us insight into the true temperament of Marylanders. The state and federal elections in Maryland from 1861 to 1867 were not free and fair because of massive voter intimidation and fraud perpetrated by the Northern army of occupation. The election of November 6, 1861 was, according to Maryland historian Thomas Scharf, "a shameless mockery" (Ibid., 460). Northern troops were stationed all over Maryland even in the areas of the state today's historian insists were "loyal." Col. J. W. Geary of the Twenty-eighth Pennsylvania Regiment arrested many "enemies to the Union," including a "candidate for senator," and positioned "detailments" of his men at the polls in supposedly Union-friendly Frederick, Buckeystown, New Market, Urbana and Sandy Hook, among other locations. "Owing to the presence of the troops, everything progressed quietly," and he was "happy to report a Union victory in every place within [his] jurisdiction" (Ibid., 459nl).

When Maryland's reconstruction era governor himself complained to Abraham Lincoln about military interference with elections in the state, Lincoln in not-so-veiled language reminded A.W. Bradford that it was this very interference at the polls that had delivered to him his governorship in 1861.[4] An 1864 referendum on a new Maryland constitution—which was contrived to silence dissent, to grant the federal government supreme power and to disenfranchise all but "loyal" citizens—was controlled by provisions set forth in the proposed document itself!⁵

The 1864 Constitution was not passed by the people of Maryland even after all of the machinations of the occupiers and scalawags, but there was a contingency plan that involved the illegal vote of Union soldiers. Presidential election scholar John T. Willis's dry commentary on the outright lawlessness surrounding the "ratification" of the 1864 Constitution sums up the state of affairs in Maryland under Lincoln's reign: "The Union soldiers vote was taken by military unit with varying methods, including *viva voce,* used in counting. Without this unusual vote the 1864 Constitution would have failed by 1,975 votes."⁶ Maryland's martial reduction by Lincoln is all the proof needed that it was neither Northern nor loyal. He saw no need for the conquest of New Jersey, Pennsylvania or New York.

Northerners were obsessed with Maryland. In a speech before a large crowd in Baltimore's Monument Square in the fall of 1863, well into the war, Salmon Chase declared that "the eyes of the whole country were turned on Maryland."⁷ The *Boston Commonwealth* editorialized that the Lincoln administration was justified in resorting to "irregularity" regarding elections in the state to "offset" the unanticipated election of copperheads in Ohio because the North was compelled to "take care that the aggregate public opinion of the country obtain[ed] recognition, somehow or other."⁸ Mob rule then was to prevail, and subsidiarity was to be a casualty of nationalist aims. The North's victory over the South would bring to fruition the fearful predictions of Patrick Henry and others and would foreshadow the worst political excesses of today's crumbling American empire.

As soon as the Yankees left Maryland, the 1864 instrument of occupation was replaced with a conservative and valid constitution. Marylanders once again expressed who they truly were at the polls rejecting Grant as did the people of Kentucky and Louisiana, states which Lincoln had won in 1864 and which had in common with Maryland the presence of Union occupiers at that time.

From 1876 (the year that a united South was starting to reassert herself) to 2004, Maryland voted most often with her sister Southern states, making a complete break with them only four times.[9] In 2008 carpetbagger-inundated Florida, Virginia and North Carolina joined Maryland in sending Barrack Obama to the White House; in 2012, sadly, he again carried Florida, Virginia and Maryland. It is Maryland, however, that has been most affected by the demographic displacement of the Southern people. It is Maryland that is increasingly isolated from her native region. Though carpetbaggers have dominated the state politically, they have still failed to destroy the Southern heart of her where secessionist-partitionist movements are gaining momentum. The departure of the state's "red" counties from the diseased I-95 corridor might yet prove Maryland's deliverance.

Trail of Lies

The Honourable Henry Wilson said, "The country had been ruled long enough by Southern aristocrats, and that his party would enforce their principles at the point of the bayonet;" and "as to Maryland, they had put the iron heel upon her, and would crush out her boundary lines." —Rose O'Neal Greenhow on remarks made to her by Senator Wilson

A few years ago I was asked to participate in the creation of a regional "Civil War" history trails project. It involved the design and placement of roadside markers that related the story of Maryland in the war and in particular the flight of John Wilkes Booth down through the boggy woods of Southern Maryland. Fully expecting that most of the people associated with the program would be the usual funny-talking liberals who dominate all aspects of life in my state, I attended two meetings ready to do battle. But I had assumed, wrongly, that they would at least demonstrate some subtlety in their attempts to reconstruct Maryland: Rather, I discovered that they were going after the state's history with a sledge hammer.

One of the participants at the kick-off meeting on the Eastern Shore announced to the group that she had learned in grad school that it was not possible to know the truth about the past. With excruciating predictability another carpetbagger took the floor to complain about the lack of attention paid to women regarding their role in American history as if this were actually the case. We hear about the role women played in history ad nauseam, ad infinitum.

At a local subcommittee meeting weeks later, I was criticized for using the term *Yankee* by a New Yorker, who has since moved to Alabama where he is no doubt posing as a Marylander and stirring up trouble, the Alabamians on whom he imposes himself all the while politely hating this interloper from "that Northern state somewhere up around Massachusetts." Another subcommittee member, a female park ranger who speaks with a generic American accent, rolled her eyes whenever I brought up the facts about the war. And there was also the deracinated local who insisted that our home county was not strongly secessionist as I had suggested and that I had failed to take into account the pro-Union inclinations of slaves and free blacks, an easily-deflated revisionist dodge that, nevertheless, is gaining favor (see "Maryland History by the Numbers"). Even if, for the sake of argument, it is allowed that black people in Maryland were unanimously "loyal" and that their sympathies by necessity must be taken into consideration when making judgments about the feelings of the general population, the same standard then must be applied to other Southern states, occupied and unoccupied, not exclusively to Maryland. But though the most cursory look at history reveals the arguments over secession that raged among white Southerners in the days prior to the war, black people, disenfranchised as they were, did not possess the power to vote for or against dissolution. They had no such power in Virginia; they had no such power in Maryland as I explained to the subcommittee (on which sat one or two individuals I respect and like). My words falling on deaf ears and my blood pressure rising, I realized then that I couldn't take any more, deciding on the spot that I had attended my last meeting.

The Civil War Trails project is now complete; the roadside markers are attractive but have little to do with what really happened in Maryland after the Yankee occupation of the state. The narrative on one marker in St. Mary's County, at first glance, doesn't seem to say anything.

> *Divided loyalties and ironies tore at Marylanders' hearts throughout the Civil War: Enslaved African-Americans and free United States Colored Troops, spies and smugglers, civilians imprisoned without trial to protect freedom, neighbors and families at odds in Maryland and faraway battlefields.*

To the extent that anyone can make sense of this sentence, it appears to weigh the assumed pro-Union sympathies of slaves and black Union troops (the latter not necessarily serving of their own volition) against the secessionist sympathies of the "spies and smugglers." The reference to "neighbors and families at odds" at home and on "faraway battlefields" (actually the battlefields were not that far away[1]) is a more useful, if unimaginative, example of divided loyalties that were, the narrative incorrectly insinuates, unique to Maryland.

Insisting on the "irony" of the Federals' jailing of civilians without due process "to protect freedom" is an inane attempt to reconcile political correctness with the truth, which I kept bringing up at those planning meetings. While the CW Trails creators at least acknowledge the detaining of Maryland citizens by the Yankee army and in doing so also hint at the inescapable truth that the North invaded Maryland, they cannot hide their taking delight in the North's crushing of a sovereign state. They assume that the union was and is indivisible and that the North was fighting to free the slaves, not to beat the South into submission and to impose a new form of government. But try as they may their stealth syntax and fancy "signage" will never succeed in altering "Civil War" history.

Joyce Bennett

Onderdonkian History

Almost two decades after Lincoln's armies crossed the Mason-Dixon Line and claimed Maryland for the North, a history text written by Henry Onderdonk was approved for use in classrooms in the city of Baltimore and in "several" counties in the state. A copy of this book was given to me by a friend, and when I received it, I immediately turned to the chapters on the War of Secession. Given the author's peculiar treatment of Maryland's involvement in that war, I was not surprised when I later discovered that Henry Onderdonk was a native New Yorker who had served as the president of the Maryland Agricultural College, the forerunner of the University of Maryland, from 1861 to 1864 (note the dates). But, strangely, according to the university's website, this Quaker carpetbagger "resigned under accusations, never substantiated, that he willingly harbored and entertained Confederate troops under the command of General Bradley T. Johnson, who had encamped on the College grounds."[1] Repentant copperhead or not, Onderdonk in his version of Maryland's history seems implicitly to affirm what he explicitly denies and vice versa. Still, in his sophistry or sarcasm, as the case may be, lies the truth.

Acknowledging the deaths of the invading Yankee soldiers while downplaying the sacrifice of the civilians who died defending the city of Baltimore in the Spring of 1861, Onderdonk describes a miraculous conversion.

> After the excitement caused by the bloodshed on the 19th of April...had subsided, an apparent change took place in the sentiment of very many who had been adverse to the use of force to restore the union; and, not a few who had armed themselves to resist the passage of the troops, volunteered in the service of the United States, or in other ways gave the Federal Government their cordial support.[2]

Almost in the same breath he details the subsequent fortification of the city by the Yankees who for some reason trained guns on their cordial and supportive "hosts."

> *When the morning of July 2d, dawned, the principal places of the city of Baltimore were found occupied by masses of artillery and infantry. The Court House, the Exchange, and many public places belonging to the city, were appropriated to the use of the troops, who thronged the streets and squares by night and by day (Ibid., 265).*

Marked by this same incongruity, Onderdonk's account of the election of 1861 falsifies the South's cause with its assumption that the Confederacy undertook a coup d'etat.

> *Notwithstanding the decided stand in behalf of the Union—which, by preserving the capital of the Republic to the Federal Government in the beginning of the war, had saved that government from total overthrow—and, notwithstanding this decided majority for the Union candidates, the administration, while calling Maryland a loyal State, acted upon the theory that she would, if supported by the Southern army, unite with the South, and press her hard with its military hand (Ibid., 269).*

Marylanders, according to Onderdonk, were not "rebels" but would have seceded if given half a chance? In spite of such contradictions the truth asserts itself: With rapidity and ruthlessness, Lincoln moved against the Old Line State because without an occupied Maryland the North might have lost the war. A loyal state by definition would not have required military coercion or rigged elections to ensure Republican victories at the polls.

Two years after Onderdonk's book was published, *Dulany's History of Maryland*, anonymously authored by "a Marylander" (Dulany being the publisher), was also approved "for the use of schools in the state." As if in response to the earlier text and its incoherent ramblings on the Old Line State and the war, *Dulany's* avoids the pitfalls of having to lie about

Maryland's essential role in it primarily by ignoring that role. Nonetheless, devoting barely a page and a half to the events that took place between 1861 and 1865, the "Marylander" who wrote the book managed in those few words to beg some weighty questions: The Union was insoluble, the Federal government supreme; what really mattered to Marylanders was that their economy not suffer from the war; all ended well.[3]

These identity-robbing mendacities are still gospel in public and parochial schools today in Maryland. Anyone who wishes to tell his children what really happened in the War of Secession, however, will find a good resource in another book published in the late-nineteenth century. In his *History of Maryland*, Thomas Scharf, whom revisionists distrust because he served in the Confederate forces, still provides the remedy for the truth hater's "tyranny over the mind."

Barbara Fritchie[1] and Stonewall

It is a mystery to me that Suzanne Ellery Chapelle's *The Maryland Adventure*, a history text used by our local Catholic school, highlights the accomplishments of "Marylander" Clara Barton,[2] in reality a Massachusetts native and Unionist who resided in Glen Echo, Maryland in her retirement years. Further, in her Barbara Fritchie narrative, Chapelle treats legend as history.[3]

> *Barbara Fritchie had lived in Frederick for ninety-three years. When she heard that Union troops were marching through her town, she waved the Union flag out her window. The troops turned out to be Confederate soldiers. Barbara continued to wave her flag to show her loyalty to the Union. A Confederate soldier saw this and warned her to take her flag inside. She kept waving the flag. Then the soldier asked his leader for permission to shoot Barbara Fritchie.*

Although Chapelle suggests that Whittier might have exercised poetic license regarding what happened following Fritchie's "patriotic" demonstration, the general impression that her text gives the student is that Fritchie had indeed waved the flag. Thus another revisionist promotes the big lie that Marylanders were mainly on the side of the Yankees, and the tradition of brainwashing Maryland school children continues. As a child, I only learned the two "uncontroversial" stanzas of our secessionist state song. As a fifth grader, I drew a picture of a log cabin in honor of Lincoln's birthday but did nothing in remembrance of Robert E. Lee on January 19. In the sixth grade, I memorized the Gettysburg Address, and, somewhere along the way, I read Whittier's poem, but it was not until much later in life that I began educating myself about the War of Secession in Maryland and discovered some interesting details about the Barbara Fritchie affair.

There is no proof that she actually unfurled the Yankee colors for Stonewall and his men to see as they were marching out of Frederick on the way to Sharpsburg. Charles T. Duvall, in *The Maryland Scene*, writes that Oliver Wendell Holmes, who "passed through Frederick" about the time that the showdown allegedly had come about, "makes no mention of it in the tale of his journey which he gave to the *Atlantic Monthly*."[4]

Whittier, defending his poem in an 1886 letter to the editor of *The Century Magazine*, declares that it was "written in good faith."

> *The story was no invention of mine. It came to me from sources which I regarded as entirely reliable; it had been published in newspapers, and had gained public credence in Washington and Maryland before my poem was written.*[5]

The youngest officer on Stonewall Jackson's staff, Henry Kyd Douglas, though he considered Whittier a "venerable poet," insisted "Old Jack" had no run-in with Fritchie, and he was at the general's side constantly when the Confederate troops were in Frederick.

> *As for Barbara Frietchie, we did not pass her house. There was such an old woman in Frederick, in her ninety-sixth year and bedridden. She never saw Stonewall Jackson and he never saw her. I was with him every minute while he was in the town, and nothing like the patriotic incident so graphically described by Mr. Whittier in his poem ever occurred.*[6]

Of course, the usual suspects will dismiss Douglas's recollections simply because he served on the "wrong" side. But his memoir has been praised even by the Yankee media. *Newsweek* called *I Rode with Stonewall* "one of the most interesting and readable personal histories of the Civil War...without partisan bile and the romantic nonsense of the novelists" (Ibid., cover). And Douglas, who in his writings is often complimentary to Northerners both civilian and military and critical of fellow Southerners, admits freely that there were both Unionist and "Southern" sentiments in Frederick. He suggests, however, that Fritchie might have been a secessionist. Regardless of her loyalties or disloyalties, she, Douglas clearly states, did not challenge Stonewall Jackson.

Furthermore, artistic license notwithstanding, Whittier's general isn't sufficiently "Jacksonian." The real Stonewall, pious and matter-of-fact, was fierce in battle but wasn't given to the terrorizing of civilians. Concerning an encounter that Jackson had in Middletown, Maryland, the same day he was said to have met Barbara Fritchie, Douglas describes the general's mild response to two young girls who were "defiantly" waving small U.S. flags in his face.

> *He bowed and lifted his cap and with a quiet smile said to his staff, "We evidently have no friends in this town." The young girls, abashed, turned away and lowered their tiny battle-flags. That is about the way he would have treated Barbara Frietchie (Ibid., 152).*

Valerius Ebert, Fritchie's own nephew, agreed with Douglas that the Confederate leader and his aunt never saw each other though he insisted she was "loyal."[7]

In his answer to Whittier, a skeptical Duvall gently chides him and suggests Fritchie's "heroism" was born of poetical fancy.

> *A splendid story and splendidly told,*
> *But does it the facts of the case uphold?*
> *The Frederick people of that grim time*
> *First heard the tale in the poet's rhyme;*
> *Of various folks who came and went*
> *Not one of them witnessed the incident.*[8]

Maryland, My Maryland

Yet fable, whether penned by poets or *Washington Post* staff writers, has long been accepted as Maryland history. In a 1995 piece on Frederick, Larry Fox properly notes that in that town "Union supporters burned cots, blankets and military supplies" so the "rebels" could not use them while "other citizens... sympathized with the Southern cause and openly socialized with occupiers."[9] And, as Fox tells us, there was a Sabers and Roses Ball held in honor of J.E.B. Stuart whose troops were camped in the area (the ball is so named because Stuart's men stopped dancing long enough to fight a skirmish close by, returning to the festivities afterwards). But, jumping the traces, Fox then begins to conflate fiction with fact, fact with fiction.

> *President Lincoln, realizing the vital role the state would play in the war, asked the Maryland legislature to hold its vote on secession in Frederick, the better to avoid any influence from the southern Maryland slaveholding planters and legislators. The legislators, minus a few Southern sympathizers that legend says were kept from entering the town, met in the spring of 1861 on the third floor of Kemp Hall...and decided narrowly to stay in the Union.*

Setting aside Fox's assumption that the legislators were asked rather than forced to meet in Frederick after Yankee troops commanded by Beast Butler had occupied Annapolis and that a sitting president ever has a right to meddle in a sovereign state's legislative matters, Fox takes several liberties with history. In September, not April, of 1861, the Yankees jailed or dispersed many of the legislators. The Federals' own records prove this. Simon Cameron himself ordered the arrests of "all, or any part of the members" of the legislature to block "the passage of any act of secession."[10] And as a result of this unconstitutional—criminal—move by the Lincoln regime a quorum was prevented.

Striking the pose of a disinterested party, Fox nonetheless favors folklore over truth. He fails to mention what Henry Kyd Douglas had written about Mrs. Fritchie, though he does acknowledge that local diarist and avowed Unionist Jacob Engelbrecht, who lived near her, never wrote a word about the alleged Jackson-Fritchie meeting. But Fox does not question that the "evidence that the tale is true is exhibited at the Barbara Fritchie Museum." In a telephone conversation with Rebecca Crago of the Frederick County Historical Society on March 28, 2013, I learned, to the contrary, that no such "evidence" exists. "Educators" and the media, nonetheless, prefer to rely on their Northern mythology: Fritchie, a true and loyal heroine of the Old Line State, did battle with Stonewall; and blue-clad celestial hosts wielding the silver sword of divine justice saved Maryland, glory hallelujah, from falling in with the Satanic reactionary slaveholders. Marylanders need to debunk such myths and to defy those who have designs on our past, to educate those who are just plain ignorant of our history.

THE SOUTHERN PERSPECTIVE ON MARYLAND

Introduction

In a 1902 speech before the Eighth Annual Convention of the Georgia United Daughters of the Confederacy, Anna Caroline Benning expresses what was then commonly assumed in the South about Maryland.

> *Georgia expended in 1901 more than a million and a half dollars on the education of her children. Yet she will receive scant honor from these children if they are to learn it from the text-books used in her schools. For example, in Eggleston's "A First Book in American History," colonial Georgia is not mentioned. The same is true of the Carolinas and Maryland, but we find eleven pages about Miles Standish, with illustrations galore.*[1]

And in her memoir, *A Slaveholder's Daughter*, Belle Kearney includes Maryland in the Southland.

> *Now, over the South, boarding schools and academies with their meagre curriculum have been supplanted by industrial institutes and colleges where young women are drilled in common-sense pursuits that will fit them to be bread-winners; sending them out into the world with skilled hands and trained minds. Medical colleges once devoted wholly to men are now equally open to women. Among these is the State Medical College of South Carolina, at Charleston, Tulane University of New Orleans, Louisiana, and Johns Hopkins at Baltimore, Maryland.*[2]

Unfortunately a feminist-progressive, Kearney, nevertheless, documents the Old South's belief that Marylanders were kinsmen, countrymen, when she remarks that in traveling "through nearly every Southern state in the interest of the Woman's Christian Temperance Union, from Delaware to

Texas," she most enjoyed visiting the home of Augusta Evans Wilson in Mobile and the Naval Academy at Annapolis.[3]

In 1861 the people of Alabama certainly did not consider Maryland Northern. In their ordinance of secession passed on January 11 of that year, an invitation was extended to Maryland and thirteen other Southern states to send delegates to a convention to be held on February 4, 1861 in Montgomery to begin the process of putting together a Southern government.

No less an authority than Jefferson Davis also counted Marylanders among the Southern people. In his two-volume *Rise and Fall of the Confederate Government*, he regrets the state's hopeless situation at the beginning of the war.

> *Maryland was the outpost of the South on the frontier first to be approached by Northern invasion....The first demonstration against southern sovereignty was to be made there, and in her fate were the other slaveholding States of the border to have warning of what they were to expect.*[4]

Laying the blame for Maryland's conquest by the Yankees at the feet of Governor Hicks, Davis, the first and only president of the Confederacy, is one of many famous and lesser-known Southerners who lived the war and who knew what Lincoln did to Maryland. Their descendants, the "beneficiaries" of public school "education" and media propaganda, may think that the Old Line State is Northern, but their ancestors knew Maryland to be geographically, culturally and politically Southern.

Mary Chestnut

Mary Chestnut, aristocratic and urbane (she considered Lincoln a yokel), in *A Diary from Dixie* does not romanticize the South, but neither does she rob us of all our cherished beliefs about it. And fortunately for students of Old Line State history, her journal offers rare perspectives on Marylanders in the Confederate army.

Mrs. Chestnut had interesting views on slavery. Calling one of its staunchest defenders "a terrible fire-eater, one of the few men left in the world who believe we have a right divine, being white, to hold Africans...in bonds forever,"[1] by the end of the war she declared, "For years we have thought negroes a nuisance that did not pay" (Ibid., 387). The race-obsessed, self-righteous white liberal of today, who patronizes and objectifies black people, will send up howls of indignation at Mrs. Chestnut's callous calculation of the usefulness of the enslaved. But her reaction to the suffering of a small boy offers a glimpse into the heart of a woman brought up in the Southern planter class long after the first African was sold to the first Yankee slaver.

> *February 16th.—Saw in Mrs. Howell's room the little negro Mrs. Davis rescued yesterday from his brutal negro guardian. The child is an orphan. He was dressed up in Little Joe's clothes and happy as a lord. He was very anxious to show me his wounds and bruises, but I fled. There are some things in life too sickening, and cruelty is one of them (Ibid., 290).*

Many peoples, many nations, down through history have been guilty of the sin of slavery, and, in fact, slavery exists today, human beings, black and white, as flawed in the twenty-first century as they were in the nineteenth.

Chattel bondage seemed to be of small concern to Mary Chestnut as defeat loomed for the Confederacy in the summer of 1864, and she despaired when she learned from her husband, General James Chestnut, aide to Jefferson Davis, that North Carolina desired to "offer terms of peace." The news, she writes, "nearly killed" her.

> *We needed only a break of that kind to finish us. I really shivered nervously, as one does when the first handful of earth comes rattling down on the coffin in the grave of one we cared for more than all who are left (Ibid., 271).*

Despite such demoralizing developments, not until the war was drawing to a close did life change dramatically for this woman of wealth and high position.

Her social circle including First Lady Varina Davis, Mrs. Chestnut, while convention still held sway and she had the means to buy the trappings of station, was relatively insulated from many of the unpleasant exigencies of the sectional strife. But reduced to rags, as Southern society was coming apart at the seams, she first experienced the bitter realities of the war as it neared its conclusion. A Southern lady in the truest sense, and therefore undefined by the material, she endured her humiliating circumstances with grace and humor.

As did Phoebe Yates Pember, she admired the Marylanders wearing Confederate gray, mentioning them several times in her diary and lauding the bravery of their ancestors during an earlier war for independence.

> *Having lived on the battlefield (Kirkwood), near Camden, we have an immense respect for the Maryland line. When our militia in that fight ran away, Colonel Howard and the Marylanders held their own against Rawdon, Cornwallis, and the rest (Ibid., 75).*

Mrs. Chestnut understood that during the War of Secession Marylanders were not always given their due by fellow Southerners. Referring to a Confederate victory in the summer of 1861, she writes, "All the eleventh-hour men won the battle; turned the tide. The Marylanders—Elzey & Co.—one never hears of—as little as one hears of Blücher in the English stories of Waterloo" (Ibid., 94-95). Interstate rivalry in the South was pronounced and likely contributed to the fact that Maryland was not always trusted or given credit for her efforts on behalf of the Southern cause. Even Rose O'Neal Greenhow did not escape criticism. Mary Chestnut, in paying homage to Maryland's Rebel Rose, also notes some undeserved resentment towards her.

> *Mrs. Rose Greenhow is in Richmond. One-half of the ungrateful Confederates say Seward sent her. My husband says the Confederacy owes her a debt it can never pay. She warned them at Manassas, and so they got Joe Johnston and his Paladins to appear upon the stage in the very nick of time (Ibid., 176).*

The people of Wilmington, North Carolina, however, recognized that debt and honored Mrs. Greenhow with a state funeral after she drowned off Cape Fear in 1864. And though Maryland's unique position in the war was not always appreciated in the South, Marylanders who fought for and aided the Confederacy were admired and vigorously defended in the highest reaches of Southern government and society, Mary Chestnut's world.

Robert E. Lee and the Liberation of Maryland

According to A. L. Long, Robert E. Lee's military secretary, "the popular air, 'Maryland, my Maryland,'" was played as Confederates crossed the Potomac in September of 1862 "with desire to wrest their sister-State... from the iron grasp of the foe."[1] The Marylanders in this army, Long writes, "felt a natural sentiment of exultation at the cheering prospect of relieving their native commonwealth from what was to them a hateful bondage." But though Lee was well-loved in Baltimore, the lower Western Shore and the Eastern Shore, he was not welcomed by all in this part of Western Maryland.

Stopping along the way to replenish depleted provisions, the army positioned itself eventually near "Fredericktown" on the eve of the Battle of Sharpsburg—an engagement that would end in a blood-drenched draw. Ten days before the battle, from the Virginia side of the river, Lee had issued his famous proclamation to the citizens of Maryland leaving no doubt as to his feelings for their state, whose "natural position," he believed, was along side her Southern sisters.

> *The people of the Confederate States have long watched with the deepest sympathy the wrongs and outrages that have been inflicted upon the citizens of a Commonwealth allied to the States of the South by the strongest social, political, and commercial ties.*

> *They have seen with profound indignation their sister-State deprived of every right and reduced to the condition of a conquered province....*
>
> *Believing that the people of Maryland possessed a spirit too lofty to submit to such a government, the people of the South have long wished to aid you in throwing off this foreign yoke, to enable you again to enjoy the inalienable rights of freemen and restore independence and sovereignty to your State.*
>
> *In obedience to this wish, our army has come among you, and is prepared to assist you with the power of its arms.* [2]

A. L. Long says this message "was coldly received" because Marylanders, though sympathetic to the Confederacy, somehow still harbored an expectation that they could remain neutral and avoid bloodshed on their sovereign ground. And there were pro-Unionists in Maryland and all over the South, even in Alabama where the ordinance of secession was not passed unanimously but by a vote of sixty-one to thirty-nine. As was the case in the highlands of Virginia and North Carolina and in East Tennessee, there was in the region around Frederick a higher concentration of "loyalists," many of whom were German immigrants or of German descent. According to Thomas Scharf, had Lee advanced into Baltimore or the "more southern counties" of the state, he would have received a warmer reception.

> *Thousands would have flocked to the standard of Lee, had they not been restrained by the Federal occupation, and by a system of espionage so zealous and so complete that it was said "that a cat could not mew in Baltimore without the fact being reported at the provost-marshal's office."* [4]

But the Confederates were not without friends in the foothills of Maryland. Writing under the pen name Personne, Felix G. De Fontaine, a correspondent for the *Charleston Mercury*, in a dispatch from Frederick reports that Stonewall Jackson was presented with "a magnificent horse... within an hour after he touched Maryland soil."[5] Personne praises the "cordial hospitality" of the local populace.

> *Along the road the farmers have welcomed the presence of our men with a sincerity that cannot be misunderstood, opened their houses and spread their boards with the fat of the land. One Marylander...fed, in twenty-four hours, six hundred hungry men, free of charge. Others have been proportionately liberal.*

Describing the "sentiment of the people" as "apparently about equally divided, " he tells the story of a woman who distributed money and tobacco to the Confederates and who, with fourteen other ladies, made clothing for them. But she confided to Personne that she hesitated to display Southern flags in her windows because she feared reprisals from the Yankees once the Confederates left.

Other Frederick residents, however, were not intimidated by the close proximity of Northern troops, and there was often wild enthusiasm for the Confederates. Henry Kyd Douglas writes that as soon as the Southerners put up their tents at their Monocacy Junction encampment near Frederick, they had visitors.

> *People—especially ladies—began to flock from town, either to get speech with or to see the four generals: it was a quartet well worth seeing. Both General Lee and General Jackson, feeling bad and with many things to attend to, kept close to their tents and generally declined to see people. General Longstreet was much more sociable, and Stuart was ready to see and talk to every good-looking woman.*[6]

Still the expressions of Southern sympathies might have been dampened by almost certain retaliation by the Yankees. There is also the question of who might have been there to greet the Army of Northern Virginia as they marched into Maryland: women, children, old men, the Enemy himself?

In spite of the Northerners and scalawags in their midst, most of the citizens of the Old Line State loved Lee. It was that affection that prompted some Maryland admirers during the war to present him with a sword inscribed with the phrase, "Aide toi et Dieu t'aidera."[7] Marylanders also presented Lee with a pair of golden spurs, on display today at Lee's birthplace, Stratford Hall. And for a century or more after the hostilities ended, they continued to hang portraits of the general over their mantelpieces and to christen baby boys Robert Lee. Only a handful of elderly or middle-aged men who wear the name can be found now in Maryland —that old tradition as well as the great Southern leader having lately fallen out of favor in the state thanks to the influence of the Yankee element.

The Angel of Chimborazo

A Low Country aristocrat, Phoebe Yates Pember served as a divisional matron at Richmond's Chimborazo Hospital from 1862 to the last days of the Confederacy. *A Southern Woman's Story* introduces us to insanely arbitrary bureaucrats, drunken doctors and the worst and best of Southern soldiery. Cut from the same cloth as Mary Chestnut, Pember, however, through her work at Chimborazo, was able to speak to the South's social and regional distinctions with greater authority than that most famous of Southern diarists, whose world was smaller by comparison and only fell to pieces as the war drew to its conclusion. And Pember's memoir contains considerable commentary on the plight of the Maryland Confederates, the South's neglected heroes. Those of us who remember them wish that Pember had been correct in predicting that "when sectional feelings shall have died away and a fair narration of the Confederate struggle be written, they will find their laurel leaves fresh and green."[1]

Unlike the feminist of modern times, Pember, a widow, drew her strength from her feminine nature and concern for others. Having enjoyed a gentle, refined life as a member of the Southern upper class before taking the position at the hospital, she had a rude awakening when called on to prepare some chicken soup for the most critical of her patients. Though she found it almost impossible to do, she managed to "cut up with averted eyes a raw bird, and the Rubicon was passed" (19). Delicate as she was in some respects, Pember was to teach both Yankee guards (when the Union army finally took Richmond) and hospital malingerers a lesson in Southern female courage. In the case of the malingerers, she indicated in no uncertain terms that she was not too timid to use her pistol, her ally, as she called it, to keep them at a safe distance from the barrel of medicinal whiskey for which she was responsible (101).

This memoir is important because it documents the crude hospital conditions of the day, the attitudes of Confederate fighting men and the desperate socializing of wartime Richmond, and because the South described in its pages is neither Camelot nor Tobacco Road. But Pember, who was Jewish, though unsentimental about Southerners never even hints at an anti-Semitic South. She was wholeheartedly embraced by Southern society though she did shock many people when she accepted employment at Chimborazo. But she believed that if she had failed to "soar beyond the conventional," had failed to abjure notions about delicacy in order to ease the suffering of "boys hardly old enough to realize man's sorrows," those who had sacrificed so much for a "holy cause," only then would a military hospital have been "no fit place for her" (105).

Of the seventy-six thousand who were hospitalized at Chimborazo, the Marylanders, more than any of the others there, seemed to have won Pember's affection. She also loved the Virginia soldiers considering them "the very best class of men in the field" (42). Though she thought Virginians in general were "untidy" and did not approve of those among their women who smoked pipes, she called them "kind hearted" and "generous"

(130-132). But she had it seems an even greater appreciation for the peculiar plight and extraordinary resolve of "her" Marylanders.

> *To a woman there was a touch of romance in the self-denial exercised, the bravery displayed and the hardships endured by a body of men, who were fighting for what was to them an abstract question, as far as they were concerned....No one with any reasoning powers could suppose that Maryland in event of success could ever become a sister state of the Confederacy (43).*

Pember was particularly solicitous of their welfare because, owing to the occupation of their state, their families could not send them necessities or visit them as freely as other Southerners visited their kin at Chimborazo. And she admired Maryland manners.

> *My hospital at present is quite empty—but has been very agreeable; made so by the presence of a dozen or more of young Baltimoreans, all gentlemen, but privates in the first Maryland, the "old Line." They were the Howards, Posts, Ridgely, etc.—and like all gentlemen were pleased and satisfied with everything I did for them. Since they have left, they have all written to me, kind warmhearted letters, and I have been overwhelmed by thanks for common services that have been paid fourfold...a thousand times without even a recognition of them (130).*

Pember, it should be noted, was as familiar with the "First Families" of Maryland as any native of the state. Southerners in those days knew their countrymen well.

The attention she paid to the Maryland boys worsened the normal and familial jealousies that existed between the Marylanders and the Virginians who were "not kind in feeling and act to their sister state (like the Georgians to So. Ca.)" (135). The Virginians resented Marylanders because many of them crossed the Potomac to take "comfortable clerkships," and bona fide Marylanders had to live down the fact that "every gambler, speculator or vagabond...to escape military duty, managed to procure...exemption papers proving him a native of their so considered neutral state" (42). The Virginians also resented the Marylanders because of their "rowdyism" and the fact that they were "always spreeing it in the city, and dancing attendance on the women." But conflict, most often just good-natured "chaffing," was not confined to natives of the Old Dominion and the Old Line State: The Georgians called the South Carolinians cowards; the "up-country soldiers...decried 'them fellows from the seaboard, who let us do all the fighting'"; the Mississippians laughed at the "backwardness" of the Tennesseans; and the North Carolinians "caught it on all sides" (47-48).

Regardless, the animosity towards the Maryland soldiers was most in evidence and exhibited even by the surgeons who found their "awkward customers" too independent and haughty. The Marylanders were aggrieved, Pember writes, by virtue of the fact that many of them though "well-born" were forced to serve as privates for the duration of the war when "less deserving" men had risen in rank (43). Even wounded and dying for the Confederacy, they were not accepted by fellow Southerners at Chimborazo for reasons not entirely clear. Maryland had not seceded, but then neither had Kentucky, and there was no apparent ill will towards the Kentuckians at the hospital. Since many of the Marylanders were Catholics (and many Kentuckians as well), it is tempting to blame religious intolerance. Pember herself, however, not typical of the Protestant South, was well loved by fellow Southerners. That feeling was mutual, though she did gently mock the hypocrisy of Yankee-despising Christians—those "for whom Christ died in vain" (123). Furthermore, Confederate Catholics were not as rare as is commonly supposed, and below the Mason-Dixon anti-Catholicism seems more a postbellum phenomenon.

Whatever the reason for their ostracism, Chimborazo's otherwise forsaken Marylanders had a strong advocate in Mrs. Pember, who followed very closely the events as they unfolded in their home state. She was especially interested in the displays of Southern patriotism on the part of the "indomitable" women of occupied Baltimore and loved receiving news of their latest fashions and their defiance of the Yankees by such rebellious acts as wearing black when Stonewall Jackson died (118-119). Taking considerable pride in her own clothing, Phoebe Pember went to great lengths to buy fabrics to sew stylish dresses and skirts in the pockets of which she could hide her firearm.

By the end of her service at Chimborazo, her "little friend" came in handy as she defended herself against those aforementioned whiskey-stealing "hospital rats." And years of tending maggot-infested wounds and assisting in countless amputations, not only left her unperturbed by the horrors of nineteenth-century medicine but also unafraid to face anything that the Yankee occupation might bring about. Her observations on the cross section of Southern society that passed through Chimborazo's doors— including her "poor outcast Marylanders"—preserve a South mis-characterized today by those who hate it and, almost as often, by those who love it.

MARYLANDERS IN THE WAR

Governor Hicks: Accidental Defender of Maryland History

As 1861 drew to a close, Governor Thomas Hicks recorded for posterity the events of the Northern invasion and occupation of Maryland in a message he sent to members of the state's first reconstruction era legislature, an extralegal body that would prove friendly to the Yankee regime. In defending his reluctance to authorize a special session of the previous General Assembly, Hicks acknowledges how close Maryland came to seceding.

> *I believed that I was thoroughly acquainted with the proclivities of a majority of the members of that Legislature. I was perfectly convinced that they desired Maryland to leap, no matter how blindly, into the vortex of Secession.*[1]

If most Marylanders had been at odds with their secession-minded representatives, as Hicks insisted, there was every reason for his welcoming a special session. Had lawmakers then moved to hold a sovereign convention, the will of Hicks's "loyal" populace would have prevailed against a separatist minority. His refusal to call together that legitimate legislature until the state was seized by Lincoln betrayed a belief that his constituents, from whom he received numerous death threats, were not in favor of the Yankees' unconditional union. The "old woman in petticoats," as one Southern Marylander referred to the governor,[2] in trying to minimize the secessionist inclinations of the electorate and to sugar coat the Northern conquest of his state, revealed instead that Maryland was on the verge of joining the Confederacy in the fall of 1861.

In late 1860 Governor Hicks, appealing to the Southern temperament of Marylanders, nonetheless assured them that Lincoln, whom they overwhelmingly rejected, posed no threat.

> *Identified, by birth, and every other tie with the South, a slave holder, and feeling as warmly for my native State as any man can do, I am yet compelled by my sense of fair dealing and my respect for the Constitution of our country to declare that I see nothing in the bare election of Mr. Lincoln which would justify the South in taking any steps tending toward a separation of these States.*[3]

Jefferson Davis in his memoirs credits Hicks for his efforts on behalf of peace observing that the governor at the beginning of the secession crisis "avowed the desire, not only that… [Maryland]… should avoid war, but that she should be a means for pacifying those more disposed to engage in combat."[4] Less a peacemaker than a fast-talking schemer, Hicks, enraging an already angry Baltimore crowd with his pro-Union remarks, hastily reverted to his Southern patriot iteration assuring his audience that he would "suffer [his] right arm to be torn from [his] body" rather than "raise it to strike" the South.[5]

As the Yankee armies continued to descend on his state, however, he reckoned it no longer advantageous to take the part of the "revolutionaries" and threw his lot in with the Northerners. To ennoble himself and rationalize a rank duplicity, Hicks employed the subterfuge that the Yankee invasion was a Providential blessing and that Marylanders were at cross purposes with their legislature. Hicks writes that he was…

> *unwilling to allow that body an opportunity so to misuse its great power; not doubting that, in imitation of the Legislature of then seceded States, it would exert that power to the great detriment of the people of Maryland.*[6]

The governor in his letter to the puppet legislature also boasts that "his" decision earlier that year to move the meeting place of the General Assembly from Annapolis to the less "disloyal" Frederick area accomplished his "full purpose": Maryland had been kept from seceding, and "bloodshed" had been "averted from her soil." Sharpsburg was to prove Hicks wrong on the second point. Justifying his actions, he explains that the ante-reconstruction legislature had "attempted to take, unlawfully, into its hands both the purse and the sword" in order to "plunge" their state into secession and was "deterred from doing this latter only by the unmistakable threats of an aroused and indignant people."

But it was not "aroused and indignant" Marylanders who brought the dissolution wagon to an abrupt halt but a governor who ignored the state constitution and Yankee soldiers who arrested a sufficient number of Maryland legislators to prevent a quorum of them to assemble.

> *Restricted in the duration of its sessions by nothing but the will of the majority of its members... [the legislature]... met again and again; squandered the people's money, and made itself a mockery before the country. This continued until the General Government had ample reason to believe it was about to go through the farce of enacting an Ordinance of Secession; when the treason was summarily stopped by the dispersion of the traitors.*

The Governor Hicks who had once pledged that he would never betray his Southern brethren, now supported Lincoln's war on the South. Jefferson Davis fully grasped the governor's inconstancy and what lay at the heart of it.

> *It would be more easy than gracious to point out the inconsistency between his first statements and this his last. The conclusion is inevitable that he kept himself in equipoise, and fell at last, as men without conviction usually do upon the stronger side.*[7]

Hicks seems to have had in mind all along a waiting game that allowed him time to determine what course served his interests. Confederate general and fellow Marylander Bradley Johnson said of the governor that he was a "shrewd" and "sharp" man who " knew that Maryland was as ardently Southern as Virginia."[8] Johnson believed Hicks "wanted to save Maryland to the Northern States" because the governor calculated that Maryland would become a more "conspicuous power" in a Northern rather than Southern nation.

Hicks's name should be as well-known as Grant's or John Wilkes Booth's because there is hardly a more fascinating—or important—figure in American history than the governor, a weak, indecisive fool, some revisionists insist, the voice of reason according to other rewriters of the past. But Hicks was an arrogant, word-parsing opportunist and a petty tyrant with big ambitions who, if he had acted in accordance with the wishes of the people of his state, would have contributed greatly to a Southern victory in the War of Secession. Because he was unprincipled and self-absorbed, his besieged Maryland eventually fell to the Union and became "a miserable and disgraced appendage" of the North.[9] Hicks left Maryland bound to a foreign land, then quickly faded into the obscurity he sought so desperately to avoid.

What Dr. Mudd Saw

(This essay appeared in the April 2011 issue of *Chronicles: A Magazine of American Culture* published by The Rockford Institute, Rockford, Illinois.)

> *"I have lost all confidence in the veracity and honesty of the Northern people, and if I could honorably leave the country for a foreign land, I believe our condition would be bettered."* —Letter to Frances Mudd, by Samuel Mudd, September 5, 1865

After shooting Lincoln, an injured John Wilkes Booth fled southward out of Washington and headed for a small plantation at the edge of Zekiah Swamp in Charles County, Maryland. Though Dr. Samuel Mudd would later declare he had not recognized the fugitive in the false whiskers at his door that Holy Saturday morning, he was, in fact, acquainted with him, having been introduced to Booth in November 1864. That same fall, "Wilkes" made at least one visit to the Mudd residence, and in late December Mudd joined Booth and John Surratt for a cup of Christmas cheer at the National Hotel in Washington. Nevertheless, though he might have seen beyond his patient's attempt at disguise, we cannot assume that Dr. Mudd knew that he was setting the leg of an assassin, or that he had ever conspired to murder Lincoln—he had perhaps plotted to kidnap the old despot, but not to kill him. Untroubled by matters of guilt or innocence and out for Southern blood, the Yankees found Mudd all too handy, as was the South's most tragic figure, Mary Surratt. His defense attorney, Gen. Thomas Ewing, dryly mocking the extraconstitutionalities of Secretary Stanton's military tribunal, delivered up to the court a "more Northern" defendant, the same reconstructed Mudd now embraced by deracinated Mudd descendants and the revisers of the Old Line State's history. But this likely operative *par occasion* in Maryland's Confederate underground, the real Prisoner of Shark Island, identified himself as a Southerner and entertained a healthy hatred for the Yankees.

His bitterness toward the Black Republican regime was rooted, however, in much more than his unjust treatment at their hands. In an 1862 letter canceling his subscription to a New York journal, Mudd refers to Yankees as "Puritanical, long faced" hypocrites who had "caused the destruction of one of the most glorious nations upon the face of the earth." Mudd was well aware of the dire implications of the South's defeat, but writing from Fort Jefferson prison in 1867, he expresses the hope that the old republic will someday be restored:

> *The New York Herald, so bitter before in its denunciations of everything Southern or Democratic, has now turned around and advocates their principles…By straws we know the direction of the wind, and we can conclude from these incidents the allaying of strife, and the return to sober reason and justice.*

The North's victory, rather, would signal the end of constitutional rule and the ascendancy of the tyrannical multitude Mudd so feared. Today, we have the spectacle of "conservative" media personalities praising the legacy of Lincoln and shouting down anyone critical of Old Abe, unaware of the inherent contradiction in their daily rants against that which he wrought.

Because most Americans—including more than a few Medicare-loving Tea Party protesters—are unversed in the ingenious, if flawed, compact crafted by the Framers, they willingly cede to the federal government many and undefined powers. As predicted by John C. Calhoun, political control is shared by two corrupt and virtually indistinct parties who vilify dissenters, court the demimonde, and govern by polls in the tradition of Lincoln's successor, Andrew Johnson, about whom Dr. Mudd writes, "The President does not feel warranted in the execution of his plainest duties under the Constitution without first consulting the mob spirit." From prison, Mudd laments,

> *Our country seems now not to be governed by the Constitution, or by law, but by unbridled popular or public opinion, of which I have no doubt many others, as in my case, have been made victims.*

As Maryland's most famous Confederate spy, Rose O'Neal Greenhow, notes in her memoirs, slavery was only a predicate of a war waged to subjugate the South and to establish a more powerful nationalist government. The peculiar institution alone did not separate the nations above and below the Mason-Dixon Line. Dr. Mudd believed that Southerners were "differently constituted," possessing a keener "sense of honor," and that Yankees were a "Pharisaical... stealthy, and cowardly" people who made "good cow drivers, pickpockets and gamblers." In January 1868, 14 months before he was to be pardoned by President Johnson, a melancholic Mudd tells his wife, Frances,

> *Nothing would afford me more pleasure than to be able to comfort & console you in your present unhappy & helpless condition. So long as the Government is controled [sic] by men without souls & less honesty I can not promise you nor myself anything. The Spirit of infidelity pervades the whole Country. This is not only in regard to God, but to the laws & the Constitution of the Country. They are materialists & think only of self-gratification—exulting in the ruin & misery they cause others.*

A century and a half later, soulless materialism still reigns in America. Dreaming of a uniracial global utopia, unholy elites alternately placate and fend off a feral underclass and manipulate the overfed and unthinking throngs in the middle: Bill O'Reilly's "the folks." Beyond all this, Samuel Mudd lies buried just off a busy highway in carpetbagger-ridden Southern Maryland at old St. Mary's Catholic Church—the place, it is believed, he first met fellow Marylander and celebrated actor John Wilkes Booth.

Confederate Rose

Had Rose O'Neal Greenhow, at the outset of the War of Secession, confounded the battle plans of the Confederates rather than those of the Yankees, school children in the Old Line State today would be reading about her instead of Barbara Fritchie. But having served the Confederacy, Maryland's Rebel Rose has been dutifully disregarded by most historians, though more recently she seems to have merited the attention of some "women's studies" types. A well-read and well-traveled woman, she shared much in common with her contemporaries, diarists Phoebe Yates Pember and Mary Chestnut, each in her own way contributing to the Southern cause. Of the three the most politically astute, Rose alone was directly involved in the prosecution of the war, the leadership of the Confederacy attributing to her in large measure the South's victory at First Manassas.[1]

Even while in captivity, this "haughty dame," as Benjamin Butler called her, continued her covert activities sending and receiving dispatches right under the noses of the Yankees. Her imprisonment began on an August day in 1861 when, as she was returning from a "promenade," she was placed under house arrest. Just moments before she was taken into custody, she swallowed "a very important note" she had concealed in her clothing. Along with her young daughter she spent five months in Fortress Greenhow, as her Washington D.C. residence was known, before she was sent to Old Capitol Prison, a bitter twist of fate in that the latter was formerly a boarding house operated by her aunt and once Rose's home. Leaving behind the rural Maryland of her childhood, as a young woman she had gone to live there for a time. Among her aunt's boarders was John C. Calhoun, the legendary champion of state rights, who "breathed his last" within the walls of Rose's future prison. He was her mentor and teacher.

> *I am a Southern woman, born with revolutionary blood in my veins, and my first crude ideas on State and Federal matters received consistency and shape from the best and wisest man of this century, John C. Calhoun. These ideas have been strengthened and matured by reading and observation. Freedom of speech and of thought were my birthrights, guaranteed by our charter of liberty, the Constitution of the United States, and signed and sealed by the blood of our fathers.*[2]

Her views on the Constitution will be more acceptable to modern sensibilities than those she held regarding slavery—unlike Phoebe Pember and Mary Chestnut she was a strong advocate of the peculiar institution. But modern sensibilities are also offended by Lincoln's real views on race and colonization. There is no doubt that slavery should have been abolished. It is immoral. But how to abolish it was the sticking point. Mrs. Greenhow quite rightly believed that it was a factor in but not the sine qua non of the war.

> *In the first place, slavery, although the occasion, was not the producing cause of the dissolution. The cord which bound the sections together was strained beyond its strength, and, of course, snapped at the point where the fretting of the strands was greatest (Ibid., 324-325).*

The Yankees invaded the South to facilitate the collection of tariffs or, that failing, to goad the South into taking the first shot, but ultimately to subjugate the Southern states, not to free the slaves. Even if, for argument's sake, all were to agree that every man, woman and child in the South were fighting for slavery, the North was not fighting to abolish it (when Lincoln needed something to rekindle war passions among Northerners, abolition, conveniently, became the purpose of the conflict—the very liberals who justifiably condemn George W. Bush for his changing objectives mid-stream in military adventures will praise Father Abraham for the same expediency). Culturally disparate, North and South were destined to clash as they were never really one.

Rose Greenhow despised the North and Northerners (though she did acknowledge kindnesses on the part of individual Yankees). Northerners didn't like "that damned Secesh woman" either, but they were nevertheless fascinated by her, her name often mentioned in the Northern papers.

Although the coarse and sometimes menacing Yankee guards made her months of house arrest difficult, Rose managed to settle down to a fairly normal routine during that phase of her confinement. The transfer to the Old Capitol Prison was almost her undoing as she and Little Rose suddenly found themselves shut up in a filthy, airless room the walls of which "swarmed with vermin." A lack of sunshine, a scarcity of food and Yankee intimidation took their toll on the health of mother and child.

Finally, after a ten-month ordeal in Old Capitol, Rose learned that she would be "exiled" to the Confederacy. She was to wait interminably it seemed for her release because of delays which she blamed on George McClellan who, Rose believed, "credited" her too often for his lack of success as a military leader. When she and her daughter were at last en route to Richmond, their first stop was occupied Baltimore. On her last day in this city, she reveled in the outpouring of affection from fellow Marylanders.

At five o'clock on the afternoon of Sunday, June 1, the officer of the guard announced that all was in readiness to depart for the boat, which had been detained for the purpose of conveying me to Fortress Monroe. A large number of persons had by this assembled to offer congratulations....

The 'good-bye' was spoken, and many friends followed to the boat....General Dix and suite being expected, the boat was detained for them several hours. During all that time, an eager

> *crowd surrounded the approaches to the wharf, and, regardless of the angry and rude repulse of the military, continued to assemble. So far as the eye could reach handkerchiefs were waving, and the tearful eye and hearty 'God bless you!' which responded from all sides, regardless of the bayonets of the tyrant, told that the hearts of the people of Maryland, however repressed and down-trodden, beat in unison with their brethren of the South (Ibid., 317-318).*

Arriving in the Confederate capital, Rose came face to face with the horror of war. But she spared no pity for the Yankee soldiers killed in the "battles before Richmond."

> *The proud triumphant foe, with every advantage of numbers, &c., in his favour, who flaunted his banner before our capital, threatening us with annihilation, was defeated and driven for shelter behind his gunboats. The scene of their insolent triumph was changed into a charnel-house, with the very air rank and pestiferous with the effluvia from their half-decomposed bodies, where they lay as a warning monument to tyrants for all future time. This is a fruitful theme for abler pens than mine (Ibid., 322-323).*

Rose remained in the Confederacy only a short while before sailing to Europe where she acted as an emissary for Jefferson Davis. It was in Europe that she wrote and published *My Imprisonment and the First Year of Abolition Rule at Washington.*

Greenhow's book might have been as William Saffire suggested "propaganda, shot through with errors" and "florid and self-serving,"[3] but she was nevertheless an effective agent for the South. Her last mission on behalf of the Confederacy, the delivery in person of an intelligence report to President Davis,[4] ended abruptly when the blockade runner on which she was a passenger foundered on the New Inlet Bar off Cape Fear. The captain allowed her to be taken ashore in a small boat, but, weighted down with English gold—the proceeds from her book—she never reached land, drowning in the stormy seas. Her grave is marked with a simple marble cross at Oakdale Cemetery in Wilmington, North Carolina. Today an unremarkable old lady who probably never met Stonewall Jackson and likely never told him to shoot her gray head if he must has come to symbolize Maryland during the war, while shamefully "so noted a rebel" and her exploits are virtually unknown in the small Southern state where she was born and raised.

Lamb to the Slaughter?

No freeman shall be fined or bound...
Except by lawful judgment found.
And passed upon him by his peers.
Forget not, after all these years.
The Charter signed at Runnymede.
—Kipling

Mary Surratt lies buried at Mount Olivet in a once-respectable, now-dangerous and poverty-stricken Northeast Washington, D.C. neighborhood. She rests there with Henry Wirz, the ill-fated commandant of Andersonville Prison, as well as several of my Maryland and Virginia ancestors. Her son John, who would have forfeited his own life if the Yankees had caught up with him sooner, walked out of a courtroom a free man just a few years after the Republican regime hanged his mother. Though her guilt or innocence regarding the Lincoln assassination will never be determined, what is a fact is that Mrs. Surratt was a sacrificial offering to a bloodthirsty mob and their new god democracy.

The United Daughters of the Confederacy once placed a marker on Mary Surratt's grave, but, removed at the request of her descendants, it was no longer there the September Sunday I visited Mount Olivet with my Aunt Elizabeth. Because her father (my grandfather) hated Catholicism (though he had married a Catholic), as a toddler my aunt was spirited away from her home in the country by kinfolk and baptized surreptitiously at St. Peter's on Capitol Hill, a church once attended by members of the Surratt family. Settling after her world travels in a nice NW D.C. area, she embodied Old Washington, a Washington not much different from the one Mrs. Surratt knew in the days before the "War of the Rebellion." When it was ended, D.C. was again the quiet tidewater town about which North Carolinian David Brinkley writes in his memoirs. Even in the 1950s and 1960s, in spite of the impact of war and cultural revolution, a politer Washington still moved to a Southern tempo. Today it has, sadly, superimposed upon it, a Yankee culture.

People from nearby Virginia and Maryland have had a long-standing tradition of working and living in the District. It was, therefore, not unusual that Mary Surratt, after the death of her husband, John, left rural Prince George's County, Maryland, where she operated a wayside tavern, to open a boarding house on H Street in Northwest D.C. It was there on April 19, 1865 that she was arrested by the Yankees.

As chronicled by Surratt biographer Elizabeth Steger Trindal, Old Capitol Prison-Carroll Annex where Mrs. Surratt was taken was a pest hole, the prisoners there forced to breathe in the mephitic air of a crude sanitation system, their clothes even reeking from the foul atmosphere.[1] A middle-aged woman at the mercy of rough turnkeys, Mrs. Surratt, in the almost unbearable humidity of a Washington summer, was to endure tribulations of a physical nature that would have driven a lesser woman insane. Though eventually removed to more "humane" surroundings, her suffering and humiliation worsened when she was first transferred to the Old Penitentiary at the U.S. Arsenal and a cell not much larger than a coffin (Ibid.,143).

To the Yankees, Mary Surratt's real crime was that she was the mother of a man who was a Confederate courier and an acquaintance of John Wilkes Booth. A far more likely conspirator, John Surratt escaped her fate because the authorities couldn't find him. Some "historians" today believe Mrs. Surratt's associations and "Southern sympathies" are proof of her complicity in the killing of Lincoln. But even if not innocent, she would have been found not guilty had she been tried by disinterested military judges.

After she was condemned to die, President Johnson failed to spare her refusing to instruct military officials to comply with a writ of habeas corpus issued hours before her execution (Ibid., 211). And Johnson ignored appeals for clemency from Mary's daughter Anna and many others. Despite efforts to save her on the part of her priest confessor, Father Jacob Walter, Mrs. Stephen A. Douglas and even condemned conspirator Lewis Powell (Ibid., 212-213), the Yankees only hardened their hearts and on July 7, 1865 marched Mary Surratt along with Powell and two others to the gallows. Elizabeth Trindal tell us that as Surratt was "helped to her feet and led to the drop," she was heard to say "Don't let me fall" (Ibid., 225).

"Chief witness" against Mrs. Surratt, Louis Weichmann, in his account of the assassination, insisted that his testimony amounted only to circumstantial evidence and did not contain anything that would have incriminated her.[2] And Weichmann acknowledged his own suspect entanglements with many of the conspirators.

> *It is a noteworthy fact that out of the ten persons who were charged by the Government as being principals in and accessories thereto, I was most innocently and unsuspectingly brought into relation with seven of them, and also with many witnesses for the prosecution and defense in the Conspiracy trial. Indeed, I regret to confess it, a strange fatality seems to have twined itself about my life in this respect.*[3]

It was not Weichmann but Mary Surratt who was to pay for the assassination of Lincoln. Stanton and his minions unjustly put to death a woman whose guilt was not properly established, but then the central government born of the "Civil War" was dictatorial and contemptuous of due process. Although it has morphed into a bland, "do-gooder" tyranny, it conceals a savagery just beneath its soft surface: It is essentially the same monstrous thing that tortured and murdered Mary Surratt.

Joyce Bennett

Who Was John Wilkes Booth?

I struck for my country and that alone...I have too great a soul to die like a criminal.

We hated to kill.
—JWB

Lincoln's assassin is popularly characterized as an insane third-rate actor who suffered from delusions of Southernness. The truth is that although his sanity is debatable, John Wilkes Booth *was* a Southerner with not inconsiderable theatrical abilities and a proud, imprudent and ultimately violent secessionist. But the no-talent blackguard and madman who turned against his "native" North and failed his legendary—and loyal—Thespian family, is the Booth favored by historians.

Terry Alford, one of the "experts" interviewed for PBS's "The Assassination of Abraham Lincoln," which first aired on February 9, 2009, seems almost to find fault with Booth's long-held and "passionate hatred for tyranny." We can only hope Alford considers this, though not a justification for shooting a president, at least an admirable personal attribute. Liberty is always in peril if despotism provokes mere mild disapproval.

"The Assassination of Abraham Lincoln" reiterates the moldy fallacy that a Marylander's fighting for the cause of the South was an aberration: Raphael Semmes sided with the South because he lived in Alabama; James Ryder Randall wrote his Southern battle song "Maryland! My Maryland!" because he was teaching school in Louisiana; and, according to James L. Swanson, another contributor to the PBS production, "John Wilkes spent most of his time in the South. That's where he received his great acclaim, that's where he felt best loved. And over time he naturally adopted the Southern point of view." But Semmes, Randall and Booth were Southern men because they were Marylanders. Booth's family might have had

Unionist leanings, but this was not unusual. There were Union people in Maryland, Virginia and all across the South. Even Robert E. Lee's kinsman Virginian Samuel Phillips Lee was a Union naval officer who participated in the blockade of Southern ports.

Not content with reconstructing history, Terry Alford mines the Booth psyche with all the analytical verve of a Jerry Springer or an Oprah.

> *There was a really big burden to being a Booth whether you went on the stage or not. You have these giants in your family that you're inevitably compared to and to some extent, as a young man, he needed to just psychologically to individualize himself from them and to show that he was his own person.*

Although one of the Lincoln kidnapping conspirators, Samuel Arnold, Booth's former classmate at St. Timothy's Hall in Catonsville, Maryland, himself came to conclude that Booth was unhinged,[1] he was initially mesmerized by him. In his memoirs, Arnold reveals his infamous friend's extraordinary personality.

> *I found Booth possessed of wonderful power in conversation and became perfectly infatuated with his social manners and bearing. Instead of gazing upon the countenance of the mild and timid schoolmate of former years, I beheld a deep thinking man of the world before me, with highly distinguishing marks of beauty, intelligence and gentlemanly refinement, different from the common order of man, and one possessing an uninterrupted flow of conversational power, in which all the characteristics of different natures were combined.* [2]

Arnold's John Wilkes Booth, who with a pistol ball apotheosized Abraham Lincoln, has been transformed into a one-dimensional character.

There is also the temptation in general to impugn Booth's acting ability—as well as the circumstances of his birth—when this should be considered independently of his crime. Booth was so striking in appearance that there is the tendency to conclude that his success in the theater was not entirely a function of the quality of his performances. He appears, however, to have been a flamboyant and undisciplined actor—one who made and spent a lot of money— who may or may not have possessed an undeveloped genius. None of this of course has any bearing on his politics or his bloody deed.

It is not going out on a limb to say that Booth was an egotist in the extreme and certainly a zealot. While many would have him play the evil maniac to Lincoln's saint, Booth might not have been so much a crazy man as someone who failed to conquer the rage tyrants engender, the rage that threatens to squelch reason in the sanest of people.

As to his compatriots, not everyone associated with Booth was a simpleton as is commonly thought. Lewis Powell was from the Southern planter class and nobody's fool. And there were others in Booth's circle who were well educated or at least intelligent men from respectable middle-class homes. They originally came together to plot the kidnapping of Lincoln intending to hold him as a bargaining chip to effect the release of Southern prisoners of war. When this kidnapping conspiracy fell apart, Booth's intentions turned deadly.

Booth regarded himself as some sort of partisan in service to the South, a "Confederate doing duty upon his own responsibility"[3] and viewed the taking of Lincoln's life as a legitimate act of war. But though Booth might have deemed the commander in chief of the U.S. forces fair game and though the conflict between North and South had not officially concluded, Booth had acted without orders from the Confederate government—and Lewis Powell's attack on Secretary of State Seward who was clearly not a combatant was nothing more than attempted murder. Succumbing to bitterness at one point, Booth writes that the South had "never bestowed upon" him "one kind word" and that had he gone to the Confederacy he would have become merely "a private soldier or a beggar" (Ibid.).

Booth believed that Southerners initially fought to preserve slavery but immediately abandoned this objective: "The South are not, nor have they been fighting for the continusance of slavery. The first battle of Bull Run did away with that idea" (Ibid.). Nonetheless, Booth believed that America was "formed for the white, not for the black man." He considered slavery to be a "blessing" for both while vowing that no one would have helped the "Negro race" more than he had there been "a way to still better their condition" (Ibid.). Obviously a product of his times as was Lincoln, whose own views on race will not withstand too close a scrutiny even by those who worship him, Booth did not hate black people in spite of his unsavory notions about them. And he objected more to the methods of abolition employed by the North than to abolition itself (Ibid.).

The most intriguing villain in the War of Secession, Booth receives little attention in his home state where, if he isn't overlooked, he is reconstructed. Those who want to Northernize Maryland's history—the ones who would love to knock down her few remaining slave cabins—will deny the real and embrace PBS's Yankee-turned-Southerner Booth. A few years ago the actor's birthplace, Tudor Hall in Bel Air, Maryland, was almost bulldozed, but, miraculously, it still stands. Preserving the boyhood home of the murderer of Lincoln doesn't seem the proper thing to do in a small Southern state attempting to redefine itself as Northern. But it is necessary to allow artifacts to speak for themselves even if they make cultural cleansers squirm.

MARYLAND: HEART AND SOUL OF THE CONFEDERATE NAVY

Admiral Semmes: Southern Born, Southern Bred

The Southern sea raider Alabama, a British-built steam sloop, took so many ships by moonlight her officers grew accustomed to a fresh newspaper everyday at breakfast compliments of a Union vessel captured the night before.[1] A product of the tobacco planter culture of Tidewater Maryland, her commander, Raphael Semmes, was once loved and hated the world over. The sinking of the Alabama by the Yankees was such an important event that the French master Édouard Manet captured it on canvas. Uncelebrated today, Semmes is too fascinating a figure to escape completely the notice of the modernist historian even as he hammers the facts about Semmes, the War of Secession and Maryland into a matrix of half-truths and outright lies.

Semmes biographer John Taylor calls the Southern naval hero a "zealot" because of Semmes's inability to see any good in the Northern cause,[2] and Warren Spencer concludes that his "philosophical mariner" was a complicated personality plagued by "conflicts."[3] Neither zealous nor all that complicated, Semmes, though an anti-abolitionist, took up arms against the North to defend his Southern homeland and the principle of subsidiarity.

Sufficiently stern as the times and the necessities of sea service demanded, he forgave desertion, however, and even afforded a sailor a "chance to desert" when he played at being the "sea-lawyer," Semmes reserving the "quids, and quos," the "pros and cons" for himself.[4] Under his command, when a ship was taken very often "the torch followed the examination of the papers,"[5] but Semmes was no pirate. His burning of enemy vessels and contraband and his general disposition of prizes, in strict accordance with maritime law and without benefit of access to home ports,[6] constituted a legitimate move of one belligerent against another.

While crediting Semmes with waging warfare "as humanely as possible,"[7] Taylor, nevertheless, insinuates a parallel between the admiral's deeds and the sinking of the Lusitania. Quoting some comments made by Wilhelm II, Taylor continues, "Two decades after the Kaiser's praise for Semmes, a German submarine would torpedo the British liner… without warning, causing the loss of twelve hundred lives."[8] Though his exploits were studied by the Germans, Semmes never sent women and children to a watery grave.

Semmes makes an easy mark for charges of villainy: He once told a Brazilian official that the South was "fighting the first battle in favor of slavery."[9] But, in spite of his advocacy of its westward expansion and his views on miscegenation, Semmes's writings indicate that constitutional matters factored into the conflict between North and South more than slavery, which issue the Yankees used later in the war to rally support in the North for their aggression against the Southern states. That Semmes's primary motivation in siding with the Confederacy amounted to a desire to preserve chattel bondage is no truer than the canard that Lincoln prosecuted the war to end it.

Warren Spencer counts as Semmes's "one great flaw" the latter's conviction "that blacks were inferior to whites" (Ibid., 210). He more generously allows that the admiral "throughout his memoirs…showed repeated instances of his devotion to individual black persons," even if guilty of a typically Southern "bifurcation of feelings" regarding their race (Ibid., 186). Spencer blames Semmes's contempt for Lincoln in large measure on Semmes's unsavory attitudes towards his African brethren (Ibid.). But the answer to Spencer's question as to why an "intelligent, kind-hearted" individual would have harbored such resentment towards the sixteenth president lies in this biographer's own argument that Semmes despised Lincoln not only because of the Confederate hero's "racism" but also because of Semmes's "interpretation of the United States Constitution." Though Spencer wrongly presumes Lincoln acted constitutionally, he correctly suggests that Semmes read the founding document strictly (Ibid., 209-210).

Taylor, assuming an originalist reading unenlightened, writes that the "law seemed to narrow rather than to expand Semmes's horizons," as if the expanding of horizons were ever the purpose of law. Taylor has little patience with Semmes's absolutism, his propensity to "develop a strong case in favor of a certain action, such as the South's right to secede, and seemingly block out all countervailing arguments."[10] This statement is prima facie evidence of a disregard for logic. In order to arrive at a "strong case" about anything, it is necessary first to render "countervailing arguments" invalid, this being the ultimate goal of discourse, reasoning and argumentation.

And Semmes did not have "tunnel vision" as Taylor believes because he defended rigorously what he had determined to be true. The burden of proving that secession is unconstitutional falls on those who put forth this premise. Taylor misses a golden opportunity to offer irrefutable evidence that dissolution is prohibited by the Constitution, managing only the weak argument that the last word on the union's inviolability is to be found in "a succession of Supreme Court decisions" that the American people exist in aggregate not as citizens of the several states.[11] Semmes would have responded to this "living" Constitution nonsense that tyranny triumphs when a federal government through the instrument of its judiciary branch becomes the final arbiter of its own powers.[12]

Replying to the challenge to specify "in what part of the Constitution" secession is addressed, Semmes answers, in his memoirs, "In no part. It was not
necessary to put it here" (Ibid., 47). The union's divisibility or indivisibility being independent of the strength of Semmes's thoughts on the issue—and they were very definite—he argues that implicit in the very creation of the union by the states is the proof that the federal government is their creature and therefore their servant.

But did the "more impulsive sisters" in the deeper South secede too soon? It is Semmes who separates the issue of the constitutionality of secession from the question of when a state should depart the union (Ibid., 52-53). He felt that the Lower South in seceding when it did had not acted rashly; Robert E. Lee disagreed. The Lower South was aggrieved by the threat Lincoln posed; the Upper South by the actions Lincoln took. Lee's resignation from the Federal forces and his joining the Confederates were symbolic of the Upper South's distress being sufficient to warrant a course that heretofore had been dreaded, secession.

Dismissive of passionate views on any subject, proponents of the now popular "balanced" approach to the war are themselves, however, rock-ribbed consolidationists and big government doctrinaires. But the Constitution, with all of its failings and the dishonesty of some of its framers, favors the secessionists, the would-be Northern secessionists in the early 1800s, the Southern secessionists in the 1860s. A state's right to secede from an illegitimate central power is an immutable moral force. Another is the principle that owning a human being is unjust. Condemn Semmes for his ideas on slavery; the fact remains that the North had no right to crush the South, to destroy the American Republic even if its motivation had been the liberation of the slaves—and it was not. Great Britain and France, after all, brought about emancipation without resorting to wholesale fratricide.

The modernist, "objective," free of the biases of those who cling to something called the truth, thoughtfully tempers his own prejudice that the South was benighted by conceding occasionally that Yankee generals had flaws. But, in spite of the worn revisionist conceit that the war is "complex," he defines this moment in American history in terms simplistic and incondite and in the end portrays the Southerner as evil, the Northerner as righteous. Never does he, however, make a solid constitutional argument for Lincoln's having provisioned a Federal fort that was situated illegally in another independent and sovereign polity.

A subscriber to De Tocqueville's ideas on the incompatibility of the North and South, Semmes believed that the two "rival nations" were destined to be parted (Ibid., 284-285). John Taylor stumbles into accuracy when he says that "Semmes's hostility toward Yankees was based in history and religion." He reaches, however, when he concludes that for Semmes the North-South conflict was a "holy war," some sort of Papist crusade against the Roundhead infidel.[13] Most Southerners—Catholic, Jewish,

Protestant—held views similar to those of Semmes regarding Yankee culture and religion.

It is true that Semmes did not like Yankee Protestant proselytizers, but the clash between Northerners and Southerners was older than America and predated the rise of Puritanism in England, the seeds of Yankee culture having been sown in antiquity in Romanized Britain, the culture of the American South arising from the Saxon heptarchy and the Celtic regions of the British Isles.

What seemed to account most for Semme's bitterness towards the Yankee was the Northerner's lack of subtlety and his ruthlessness.

> *The savage is full of prejudices, because he is full of ignorance. His intellectual horizon is necessarily limited; he sees but little, and judges only by what he sees. His own little world is the world, and he tries all the rest of mankind by that standard. Cruel in war, he is revengeful and implacable in peace. Better things are ordinarily expected of civilized men. Education and civilization generally dispel these savage traits. They refine and soften men, and implant in their bosoms the noble virtues of generosity and magnanimity. The New England Puritan seems to have been, so far as we may judge him by the traits which have been developed in him during and since the war, an exception to this rule. With all his pretensions to learning, and amid all the appliances of civilization by which he has surrounded himself, he is still the same old Plymouth-Rock man, that his ancestor was, three centuries ago. He is the same gloomy, saturnine fanatic; he has the same impatience of other men's opinions, and is the same vindictive tyrant that he was when he expelled Roger Williams from his dominions. The cockatrice's egg has hatched a savage, in short, that refuses to be civilized.* [14]

Southerners today will recognize Semmes's pretentious, university-trained but unlearned Yankee because he is alive and well, just having blown in from the North, strutting and crowing about his "superior education."

Taylor, with unintended humor we can only assume, accuses Semmes of "bias and stereotyping" simply because he recognizes a Yankee face, a Yankee accent in the commander of the Martaban, a prize that fell to the Alabama. Taylor is unnecessarily offended by Semmes's stating of the obvious objecting that his comments are somehow unfair to the Northerner.[15] No real Southerner, unless he is deracinated, would ever take umbrage at being identified as a Southerner or having his features described as Southern. To the contrary, he would be proud.

But Semmes, though he had as much dislike for the "shoddyites" and "nouveau-riche plebeians" of New York[16] as for the people Down East, did not hate Yankees and referred to them as former friends (Ibid., 127). He could not resist, however, mocking the Northerner, whom he described as "at once a duck, and a chicken" (Ibid., 481), even as he complimented him on his adaptability to both water and land. And he had every reason to hate the dishonest methods the Yankees employed in recruiting "the canaille of Europe to throttle liberty on the American continent" (Ibid., 623).

Semmes wasn't turning on his own people. He was anything but a copperhead, an inconstant "Northerner" who had embraced some new Southern identity and patriotism. And his loving Alabama, a state to which he had moved in 1841, did not mean he disparaged the land of his birth as somehow foreign.

> *I did not doubt that Maryland would follow the lead of her more Southern sisters, as the cause of quarrel was common with all the Southern States, but whether she did or not, could make no difference with me now, since my allegiance, and my services had become due to another state (Ibid., 75).*

In spite of the Yankees' having descended on Maryland early in the war, the Southern government held out hope for a time that she would join the Confederates and passed legislation exempting her vessels from capture (Ibid., 178-179, 529). Semmes regretted that the Old Line State was never able to secede (Ibid., 465, 529).

Taylor seems to be confused as to why Semmes fought for the South: He classifies Semmes (and Maryland) as Southern[17] but ascribes Semmes's loyalty to the South not to his nativity but to his relocation to Alabama.[18] Contradicting himself as well, Spencer, who calls Semmes a "gracious Southern gentleman"[19] and, concerning race relations, a victim of "his own heritage" (Ibid., 20), disregards Semmes's Southern birth in favor of dramatic narrative effect.

> *Most of his navy service had been in the South—Florida and Virginia—and having his family with him in Alabama was a kind of symbol of passing for him: He ever afterwards considered himself a citizen of the state of Alabama. Later, to provide his children with better educational opportunities, he moved the family to the city of Mobile. He bought three household slaves to help Anne Elizabeth with their growing family. Raphael Semmes was now committed to the Southern way of life (Ibid., 13).*

Spencer, inexplicably, supposes that Semmes's residing again in Maryland though only temporarily might have caused him to repudiate his "acquired" Southernness, his "Southern and Alabama mind-set" (Ibid., 84).

Many thousands of Marylanders who had never lived a single day in Alabama served the Confederate States of America. A New Yorker in the Confederate forces was a curiosity; a Marylander was not. While it is true that Semmes himself gives the impression that he was leaving the North for the South when he describes pine woods on fire near Montgomery as "peculiarly Southern" and speaks of returning to "my home, and my people," Semmes did not ever think of himself as a Northerner. He set himself apart, as Southerners do to this day, from Yankees living in the South.[20] In all likelihood he meant by his home, his people, the state of Alabama and her citizens to whom he had transferred his affections after two decades.

But neither his adoption of Alabama nor his romanticism, as Taylor would have us believe, gave him his love of the Confederate cause,[21] his affection for the South, a land that in his eyes had degenerated by the end of the war. His ship succumbing to Yankee guns off Cherbourg, France in June of 1864, Semmes lamented that she "had gone to her grave none too soon."[22] His Southern pride and honor, affronted by the South's degradation, were not virtues Semmes developed in the Heart of Dixie. They were inherited by him from those who had settled the Western Shore of the Chesapeake Bay long before there ever was an Alabama, ship or state.

Admiral Franklin Buchanan: Reluctant Confederate?

In February of 1862, Franklin Buchanan received orders to assume command of the South's James River forces, his flagship the ironclad Virginia. Portrayed as a Northern turncoat, Buchanan was in truth a Southern constitutional unionist who, perceiving that his state was a hopeless captive of Lincoln's armies and that the South was in need of aid, ultimately chose to fight for the Confederacy.

In April of 1861, convinced that Maryland was going to secede, that "she was virtually out of the Union,"[1] Buchanan presented a letter of resignation to Secretary of the Navy Gideon Welles. Not long after the gunfire and bloodshed in Baltimore on the nineteenth, he made himself available to Maryland's Governor Hicks to assist him in driving "from the shores" of Maryland "any invasion of her soil by...Northern enemies."[2] Hicks, whom Buchanan called a " vile traitor,"[3] never replied.

Compelled to leave the U.S. Navy to "follow the fortunes" of Maryland, when he later realized that his state was "tied hand and foot, literally in double irons," he rescinded his resignation.[4] Ignoring this, Welles dismissed the Naval veteran of forty-seven years. Remaining for a time at his Eastern Shore plantation, The Rest, Buchanan hoped for a "reconciliation between the North and the South,"[5] intending to request an overseas assignment in the unlikely event of war[6] because he could not have "act[ed] against the South."[7] But as the North's "coercive policy"[8] continued, he abandoned this plan and made the decision to join the Confederate forces.

Declaring that he was "no Secessionist"[9] and early on criticizing "the extremists of both sections,"[10] Buchanan, however, held what seem to be inconsistent political opinions. While he affirmed that the states had no right to secede, he believed that the central government had no right to prevent their departure.[11] And condemning the Yankees as revolutionaries,[12] he recognized the right of revolution,[13] a much more drastic course than the one chosen by the Southern states.

But whatever his ideas on dissolution and revolt, he was, in the end, to stand with the Confederates. Handling his subject with the de rigueur cynicism and self-righteousness of most of those who discourse today on Southern historical figures, Craig Symonds implies that Buchanan was a schemer and, rather than devotion to the South, his motivation for serving the Confederacy boiled down to hurt feelings and a desire to be part of "great events."[14] Symonds, who presumes incorrectly that the Confederates sought the overthrow of the federal government,[15] believes that Buchanan's desire to help the seceded states might have amounted to his settling for a lesser cause as he still smarted from the North's rejection of him. And it is true that even fellow Southerners questioned Buchanan's sincerity and secessionist credentials which he defended in a letter to the *Richmond Examiner*.[16]

Regardless of his reasons for allying himself finally with the "departed sisters," Buchanan behaved as did Robert E. Lee at the outset of the war: Lee opposed secession but resigned his commission because his first loyalty was to his state. It was the rare Southerner who did not love his state above country—in fact for each man, Lee and Buchanan, his state was his country.

That "vile traitor" Governor Hicks was not any less convinced than was Buchanan in the Spring of 1861 that Maryland would soon secede. The Yankees knew as well that they had to move quickly to take Maryland. Buchanan biographer Charles Lee Lewis argues that of the border states Maryland "came nearest" to joining the Confederacy and that sentiment there "was very strong against the aggressive and uncompromising policy of the abolitionists."[17] His state having been conquered in a matter of weeks, a stunned Buchanan can be forgiven for a brief disparagement of her as undeserving.[18] But, regardless, decrying her conquest, this "reluctant" Confederate, clearly identifying himself as Southern, did not go to war against Maryland but against those who had invaded her.[19]

Symonds accuses Buchanan of being at once stubborn and facile. Ever contextualizing and infinitely shading the "truth," relativists don't like absolutists such as Buchanan. Echoing what John Taylor had to say about Maryland Confederate Raphael Semmes, Symonds considers a shortcoming Buchanan's "tendency to choose a side and defend it with unwavering commitment," and, applying an overworked revisionist construct, laments that in the "universe" inhabited by Buchanan, "there was little room for nuance."[20] Not surprisingly, there is little nuance in Symonds's certainty that Buchanan was fighting on the wrong side.

But, then, this stubborn Buchanan, who was, according to Symonds, "in his personal life...something of a Puritan" (Ibid., 133), a label that has been applied as well to Raphael Semmes, was somehow swayed to a "more Southern" point of view, succumbing to an increasing sectionalism and developing what Symonds terms an "ironic" resentment "toward all things northern." The irony lay, he "reasons," in the "fact" that Buchanan once "celebrated 'Yankee' victories over foreign foes" (Ibid.) and that Buchanan was at heart a good Yankee with a healthy "disgust at any evidence of human weakness—drunkenness, licentiousness, even simple greed" (Ibid.). This is a textbook example of the logical fallacy.

Setting aside that most Confederates once loved the old union, and setting aside also the insulting implication that Southerners are debauched drunkards, Buchanan's strict standards of conduct were not atypical of the Southerner who valued propriety but tempered it with courtesy and hospitality. His being straight-laced was far from evidence of Northern sensibilities. And Buchanan as a seafarer understood that human weakness in the form of the social and behavioral pathologies of crew members could take a particularly sinister turn in the middle of an ocean. He of necessity was an exacting naval leader, but he was known for his good manners and charm. He was no Yankee.

Still Symonds insists on a once-Northern, *bien pensant* Buchanan who fell victim to the corruption of the "quirky" Southern culture of "geographically isolated" Talbot County on Maryland's Eastern Shore. He writes that "Buchanan forswore the legacy of his father's opposition to slavery and embraced the proslavery doctrines" of his wife's kinsmen, who owned seven hundred slaves, among them at one time Frederick Douglass (Ibid., 37, 41, 130).

Nannie Lloyd Buchanan's father, Edward Lloyd, might have been an evil man but had he been a saint, the immorality of slavery remains a separate consideration from the magnanimity or lack thereof in the slave master. Lloyd might have been unusual among border state slaveholders in his treatment of those in bondage, but his Talbot County and Eastern Shore were not, as Symonds tells us, somehow distinct from the rest of Maryland (Ibid., 41). His assertion that the election results of 1860 demonstrate that Talbot was somehow "more Southern" than other counties is baseless. There was nothing remarkable about the fact that Lincoln only received two votes in Talbot. Taking no county in the state, he received only a tiny percentage of the popular vote (see "The 1860 Presidential Election in Maryland").

Possibly believing that Maryland was New Jersey with bizarre pockets of wild-eyed secessionists here and there, Symonds downplays what happened across the Old Line State during the "Civil War": He virtually ignores the invasion and occupation of Maryland. The state, in truth, had been bound forcibly to the Union, had not lovingly embraced it, and when the Yankees went home, as if a switch had been thrown, had "reverted" to her Southern ways.

The man who commanded the Virginia at the Battle of Hampton Roads and the Tennessee at Mobile Bay was a product of the Old South, the First South of Tidewater Virginia and Maryland. Buchanan's graciousness, sense of honor and views on liberty were not affectations. He eventually won the hearts of his fellow Southerners, Jefferson Davis himself having the highest regard for Buchanan and visiting him at The Rest soon after the president was released from Fortress Monroe in Virginia.[21]

The North had no love for Buchanan. Horace Greeley condemned the appointment of the admiral to the presidency of the Maryland Agricultural College.

> *He...has just been provided with a good office by the Maryland 'Conservatives'. We haven't heard of their giving any to a one-legged Union soldier or sailor, but we hope they will all get along somehow. It is well that they don't depend for a living on the generosity or the loyalty of Maryland.*[22]

In response, the *Mobile Tribune* praised "the true hero of the Battle of Mobile Bay" and "Democratic Maryland" for wisely honoring a native son of such "indomitable spirit" calling Buchanan's political philosophy "truth itself."[23]

Buchanan loved the old constitutional union and the old flag, but he could not remain loyal to the nationalists who were seeking to dismantle the republic. His desire to preserve slavery, understandably repugnant to the twenty-first century person, cannot fully explain the course he took. Slavery was not outlawed in Maryland by the Northerners and their puppets until well into the sectional strife. As a Southerner his dilemma was what to do when the state he loved had fallen to the Yankee nation, and that nation was at war with everything he held dear. To argue that he would leave the mellow comforts of old Washington and Eastern Shore society at his age to serve in the heat and horror of an infernal ironclad clanging and banging with shot and shell for anything but profound purposes or because he had some superficial attachment to the South is to misinterpret this Confederate hero and his war. Biographers are free to despise—or to love—Buchanan, but they are not free to misrepresent him.

The Marylander on the Hunley

And how can a man die better
Than facing fearful odds
For the ashes of his fathers,
And the temples of his gods?
—Lord Macaulay

Joseph Ridgaway died on board the primitive submersible H. L. Hunley, which lay at the bottom of the sea for almost 140 years before it was raised. In the spring of 2004, in traveling to two Southern towns to honor the memory of this naval hero from Maryland's Eastern Shore, I found myself defending his birthright as well as my own.

In late March I drove to Frederick, Maryland for the Sons of Confederate Veterans' memorial to Ridgaway. Situated in the piedmont of the Blue Ridge Mountains not far from the Mason-Dixon Line, Frederick, home to many federal workers who commute to D.C., has almost lost its Southern personality, but the Battle Flag is still flying there, and its residents continue to speak with "local" accents though they are often drowned out by Yankee voices who call Frederick "Fredneck" (in reality a compliment). The Frederick area's history also reveals its former Southernness. Of the 7,333 votes cast in Frederick County in the 1860 presidential election, 103 were received by Lincoln, 437 by Douglas. And during the War of Secession, the Yankees found it necessary to interfere in elections in this so-called Republican stronghold.

Owned by historian and author David Hartzler, the funeral home where the memorial was held is located just outside Frederick in Libertytown. In the parlor, the primitive coffin containing Ridgaway's "remains" was flanked by gray-uniformed SCV sentries. All the pomp of the Charleston funeral the next month, not surprisingly, was to provide a sharp contrast with what took place in Libertytown that Saturday. The Washington area media paid only perfunctory attention to this tribute to a man who was part of a cardinal event in the history of arms because that history was Confederate— the "wrong" history. And, more to the point, it was that embarrassing Maryland Confederate history that keeps surfacing in spite of the best efforts to let it moulder quietly somewhere out of sight. The D.C. media would have run story after story about Ridgaway had he been a Union submariner and his attack vessel a Yankee *unterseeboot*.

Most of those attending the Maryland memorial ceremony seemed to have been real Marylanders. To his credit, a transplanted Georgian was also there. Though he came to show respect for Ridgaway, to the Georgian, he was an anomaly, a Yankee somehow caught up in the mission of the doomed Southern submarine. After a brief conversation, I had the feeling that he wasn't going to change his mind about my state or my people in spite of my defense of both. To him, we were the Northerners among whom he, the Southerner, had found himself.

About two weeks later, fully expecting attitudes similar to the Georgian's, I drove to South Carolina. As it turned out, I did not attend as I had planned the Hunley funeral at Magnolia Cemetery but did make a visit to the Cathedral of St. John the Baptist on the day the crew lay in state there, each man's coffin covered in a Second National Flag. On April 17, I was one of many hundreds who gathered at the Confederate monument at Charleston's White Point Gardens.

That Saturday morning Confederate colors flew from flagstaffs and balconies, from speedboats in the harbor and even from a plane overhead. Admiring one red-draped mansion, I wondered how many of Charleston's old homes had been bought up by carpetbaggers. Just before the memorial was commenced, a Yankee woman in spandex had disturbed the Southern crowd jogging through them with determination and instructing people to "excuse her" which, translated, means "get out of my way." In spite of the carpetbaggers who are now calling the city home, during the commemoration, when one of the speakers, a native, told the assembly that he was blessed to have been born in Charleston, I envied him his good fortune. The speeches I heard were moving, but I appreciated most the bagpipes and drums, the regimental bands and the martial music that had once inspired in the Southern soldier the easy courage that soon evanesces or hardens on the battlefield. Watching the re-enactors and

Southern heritage groups strike out on their four-mile march to Magnolia Cemetery, I decided to end my visit on this consummate note and to head back to Maryland grateful to have been in Charleston for any reason and certainly for this historic moment.

In their reporting on Charleston's honoring of the Hunley crew with a state funeral, carpetbagger-staffed newspapers seemed to consider it altogether remarkable that something Southern was occurring in a Southern town. And they could not resist interjecting not only the obligatory mention of the "controversy" stirred up by anything connected with Southern heritage but also the usual misinformation about the South. AP correspondent Bruce Smith, on April 18, 2004, writes that "only two" of the Hunley crewmen "were from the South."[1] In fact, three Southern states were represented on board the Hunley: Virginia, North Carolina and Maryland. We can induce from his words that Smith classifies Maryland as Northern.

Some people said that Ridgaway and the others should have been left in peace in the sea-mud that was their tomb and that the Hunley state funeral was commercial and tacky. But there is no essential difference in the burial of the crew the day they died or their burial 140 years later. There will always be those who capitalize on the sacred—this is human nature.

And I could not have missed the opportunity to remember Joseph Ridgaway; it was my obligation. Though no one in Charleston that weekend called me a Yankee to my face, nevertheless, I found myself explaining to new acquaintances why as a Marylander I was there, and I learned later when I was back home that one of Ridgaway's pall bearers, a Baltimore native, was coldly received at least on one occasion. Condescending to their more distal brethren and asserting parochial superiority, some in the South are deceived by the lies that Yankees accept and propagate. It is a pity that many Southerners know so little about their own Southland.

Joyce Bennett

Issac Mayo Unreconstructed

What urban print media "savants," Lincoln apologists all, have to say about the North-South conflict in Maryland does not hold water: It is glibly posited and riddled with contradiction. While mentioning briefly a few facts about the early days of the "rebellion"—a bone thrown to "reactionaries" who insist on real history—two *Baltimore Sun* staffers, writing eight years apart, treat almost identically the subject of Issac Mayo. Relying on the Maryland-was-really-Northern template, they create a Mayo who is a "Southern sympathizer," not a Southerner, a tragic figure unfairly disgraced but finally "rehabilitated" almost a century and a half after his death.

Carl Schoettler, in a piece that appeared in the *Sun* on August 11, 2003, chronicles the attempts of Mayo descendants to "clear" their ancestor's name.[1] He writes that Mayo was "from southern Anne Arundel County where Abraham Lincoln received just three votes in the election of November 1860." Though he parenthetically notes that Lincoln received a combined total of only nine votes from four other lower Western Shore counties, Schoettler fails to mention the fact that in Maryland, of almost ninety-three thousand votes cast, only about two thousand went to Lincoln, apparently trying to give the impression that secessionism was just an eccentricity of a small number of "treasonous" trouble spots in the state. And secessionism was what tarnished Isaac Mayo's otherwise spotless military record, Schoettler more than suggests, presuming that it was Mayo's "Civil War stance" that sullied his "good name."

Schoettler at least allows that Mayo's state "teetered on the brink of secession." But he stops short of acknowledging Lincoln's outright invasion of Maryland, referring to the citizens who defended Baltimore against Yankee troops on April 19, 1861 as a "mob" and alluding only to martial law in Annapolis when it was imposed all over the state as Lincoln's men swept down on Maryland. Schoettler sees irony in Mayo's opposition to the Lincoln government considering the heroism of Mayo's father in the Revolutionary War. Mayo's resigning from the U. S Navy, however, because he hated tyranny was in the tradition of his father and the sublimest act of a long career.

In his late sixties, Mayo tendered his resignation on May 1, 1861. His great-great-grandson Thomas Henry Gaither Bailliere Jr., along with other family members, argues that on the day Mayo died, May 10, he was still in the Navy since he had not yet been officially discharged, a factor that became the linchpin in Bailliere's campaign to "vindicate" his great-great-grandfather. Mayo's date of death is in dispute: Church records indicate that it was May 18. But his descendants, undeterred, insist that this is of no importance as even if Mayo had died on that later date, the dismissal order was signed the same day and there would not have been sufficient time for the required hand-delivered notification to reach him.

Fleshing out Schoettler's earlier article, the *Sun's* Jonathan Pitts, in his 2011 piece on Mayo, makes many of the same arguments and, to his credit, also works in a sentence or two about Lincoln's arresting of Maryland's secession-minded "officeholders" and his closing down newspapers "considered disloyal."[2] Pitts correctly adds that Baltimore was also under martial law. But Mayo's "legacy" was not as Pitts would have it one "fraught with paradox," a legacy defined by Pitts in awkwardly unparallel terms: "Union and South, Land and sea. Brash yet unknown." There would only be "paradox" in Mayo's actions had he been a consolidationist Yankee, but he was a Southerner who had served the U.S. flag devotedly and then, as thousands of other honorable Southern professional military men, had refused to support a newly despotic government's aggression against the Southern states.

Pitts concludes that Naval officials eventually expunged Mayo's dishonorable discharge designation, Bailliere having originally requested that his ancestor's record be changed to indicate that he had resigned. Schoettler, gushing that the commodore's "honor is finally restored," writes, however, that officials ruled that Mayo "died while on the rolls of the Navy." An email received by this writer on February 3, 2012 from the Naval History and Heritage Command confirms that this is indeed what his record now reads.

But a capitulation by the Navy that Mayo voluntarily left or a hair-splitting decision to place him back on the rolls is of no consequence. What must be looked at is Mayo's letter of resignation to Lincoln. By that letter he performed a sacred duty. Even if it could be determined that Mayo committed suicide, as many believe, his reasons for doing so remain unfathomable. The rightness or wrongness of his reaction to Lincoln's coercion must be considered independently of the manner of his death.

Mayo's dismissal is only disgraceful in light of the presumption that the South sought the overthrow of the federal government; the South had no right to leave the union. Neither is true. Admiral Mayo knew this. The Navy's recognition of the mere technicality of Mayo's having died before a message-carrying courier reached him has no inherent moral implication. If there be any shame associated with the commodore's name, it is to be found in his having lost his place in his state's history, in the fact, as both Pitts and Schoettler reveal, that the residents of the community of Mayo, Maryland, with a few exceptions, know nothing about him.

MORE ON HISTORY

Lloyd Tilghman and the War in the West

Because Southerners associate certain family names with specific areas of the South, when I first came across George Lloyd Tilghman, I knew that he had at least some sort of connection to Maryland or Kentucky or both. And I was correct. Although biographer James W. Raab calls the Maryland native a "forgotten" hero, he is well-remembered in the Blue Grass State (and in Mississippi too). One of the principal players in the western theater of the War of Secession, if this Confederate general is forgotten by anyone it is his own people.

At Vicksburg National Military Park there is a monument dedicated to a sword-brandishing Tilghman fighting at the Battle of Champion Hill. The Northerner will consider the memorial mawkish, and it might be, but even if the Southerner in his heart agrees, he will take an oppositional pride in it anyway.

Tilghman died horribly, receiving a fatal wound while helping some Mississippians sight a howitzer. Extraordinarily outnumbered, Tilghman and his men were charged with holding back the Yankees while the remainder of the army could be moved in the direction of Vicksburg. As he was sighting the gun, a "piece of an incoming exploding Parrot shell...struck Tilghman in the upper part of his stomach" and "nearly cut him in half."[1] Mercifully, he lost consciousness and never regained it. Highly regarded by his subordinates, he was, as we say today, a "hands-on" commander and a rash one according to biographer Bryan Bush.

> *Tilghman displayed great courage towards the Union forces, but...forgot that he was a Brigadier General who was ultimately responsible for the command of his troops. By dismounting his horse and manning a cannon, he had reduced himself to a regular soldier, but the Southern notion of honor and courage guided Tilghman's actions. When Tilghman was killed in battle, he was automatically assured a place in the annals of Southern*

*martyrdom, where courage and bravery were more important than wise and sound leadership.*²

To the contrary, the South set a premium on "wise and sound leadership," but it had, however, little more than courage with which to defend itself against the wealthy and industrial Northerners whose ranks were swollen by tens of thousands of hungry young Europeans. (The Southern army had foreigners in it, but not the high numbers the Yankees recruited. Yankee ports were not blockaded.) If Southerners had not proved themselves "too brave," the Confederacy would have collapsed in months if not weeks. The Yankees had assumed it would, until, after a surprising rout at First Manassas, they were disabused of the notion, wisely scrambling back over the bridge to Washington D.C.

And had Tilghman not fallen at Champion Hill those who criticize him for his recklessness might have praised him for his morale-building demonstration of valor. For the independent Southern soldier, exhausted, louse-ridden, his ribs showing from starvation (and his horse too weak from the same affliction to walk or pull a wagon), one bravely impetuous superior officer was more inspirational than all the aloof and tough-talking generals in the world.

Earlier in the war, Tilghman had been criticized not for possessing too much courage but for a lack of it.³ He was blamed by some in the South for the fall of Fort Henry on the Tennessee River which eventually led to the Yankees' taking Fort Donelson on the Cumberland River. But at Fort Henry, in the tradition of the Maryland 400 during the American Revolution at the Battle of Long Island, Tilghman stood his ground against impossible odds holding the fort long enough for the Confederates to fall back to the Cumberland.

Tilghman's capture by the Yankees, unfortunately, left Fort Donelson in the hands of less capable men. Had he been able to make his escape to Donelson at this critical juncture or had command there risen to the occasion, that momentous defeat, Bush theorizes, might have been avoided.⁵ When Donelson fell, the way was cleared for Yankee control of the

Mississippi and the eventual fall of Vicksburg in early July 1863, an unhappy time for the South in both theaters of the war.

The man whose death had such serious implications for the Confederacy was born near Claiborne, Maryland in 1816. Tilghman, a West Point graduate and a civil engineer, moved to Paducah, Kentucky in 1852 and was living in this area when the war broke out. Today visitors to the town will find both a museum and a monument in honor of Tilghman (as well as a high school named for his wife, Augusta). But I have not come across in Maryland even as much as one of those kudzu-covered state highway administration road markers people drive by intending to read someday.

A Distant Defender of the Old Line State

If circumstances lead me, I will find where truth is hid, though it were hid indeed within the center. — *Hamlet*, act 2, sc. 2

The tumult of the "Civil War" centenary decade presented South-haters and American empire apologists an opportunity to dominate the debate on the causes of the great national schism. Though the sixties ushered in a new virulent revisionism, it was merely a reinvigoration of the lies born of the Union's triumph over the South, the victors having spread their falsehoods far and wide since 1865. And if by this era lying about the war was nothing new, then neither was the defense of the truth about it. Taking a stand at the beginning of the twentieth century against reconstructionists who could not resist fictionalizing even Maryland's colonial days, Hester Dorsey Richardson, in her *Sidelights on Maryland History*, mentions the War of Secession almost in passing. But, in her narration of events from the founding of her state to more modern times, she assumes that she is a Southerner, that Maryland is part of the South.

Joyce Bennett

In this compilation of articles she wrote for the *Baltimore Sunday Sun* from the spring of 1903 to December of 1904, Richardson objects to the Yankeefying of her state and the egalitarian myth that Maryland was settled by convicts and Roundheads and therefore lacked Virginia's Cavalier class. Maryland was, she writes, as pedigreed as the Old Dominion, and Annapolis was once so civilized a town it was known as the Athens of America. Though charitable towards Northerners, Richardson considered them and their region foreign.

And she was incensed by obvious attempts to confuse Maryland colonists with the Plymouth Rock pilgrims. She found particularly disturbing some revisionist art on display in the Baltimore Courthouse.

> *What possible lesson can that decoration impart to our Maryland youth or to the stranger within our gates?...In the... painting there are three Puritan figures and near to the shore two big ships....The picture is positively absurd as illustrative of the settlement of Maryland and should be wiped off the canvas or sold to Boston, where it would find its proper setting.*[1]

Concerning herself primarily with that earlier Maryland history so poorly interpreted in the mural, Richardson devotes little space to "The Late War," touching only briefly on the Yankee occupation. She may have been shying away from the subject, but, nevertheless, she clearly wanted no part of the North or of Northern culture.

Imagine today an unreconstructed Marylander writing a column for the now-progressive *Baltimore Sun*. As that courthouse painting so disliked by Richardson illustrates, Old Maryland had been giving way to New Maryland long before the 1960s, but it was these years that saw the beginning of a markedly steep cultural decline. A century removed from Richardson's world, how meekly and stupidly we have allowed outsiders and the detesters of our heritage to tell us who we are.

The Maryland SCV: Keeping Watch

On May 22, 2004, the Wallace Bowling Camp of the Sons of Confederate Veterans dedicated a Cross of Honor in the name of Michael Stone Robertson, killed at the Battle of Cross Keys. And I was invited to attend the ceremony. Weekend after weekend SCV members hold many such memorial events across the Old Line State as they work to preserve Maryland's Confederate history.

Discovered a few years ago by SCV member Jim Dunbar, Robertson's final resting place is located in Bel Alton just across the Potomac from Virginia's Northern Neck. The haunt of fugitive John Wilkes Booth, this part of Charles County was a center of Southern intrigue during the war. And its rundown motels, gas stations and restaurants, many vacant, along a weedy stretch of U.S. 301 give no hint of the green hills and wisteria-covered tobacco barns that lie beyond the blight. Its past shrouded in peaceful obscurity, this corridor was saved from further development by the construction of Interstate 95 and the outlawing in the 1970s of the slot machines that had for years attracted dissolute gamblers from up and down the East Coast. As traffic on the old "dual lane" fell off, businesses dried up.

While driving down a Bel Alton back road not far from the site of Blenheim, home of Robert E. Lee's Maryland kinsmen, former Bowling Camp commander Dunbar noticed headstones on a rise of land in the middle of a cornfield. With the permission of the owner of the farm, he subsequently returned with his wife, Connie, and SCV associates to clear away weeds and to restore an ancient graveyard containing five tombstones including Robertson's and that of Samuel Hanson, father of John Hanson, America's first president under the Articles of Confederation. There are those who believe that John Hanson himself is buried in that tiny cemetery where the "Sons" gave Robertson such a fitting ceremony complete with a cannonade that served as a jarring reminder of what was demanded of those who soldiered in the War of Secession.

SCV members and their families spend much of their free time away from home in similar pursuits. In recognizing Robertson and the other Confederates from the Old Line State, they honor their ancestors and keep historians honest. Though the fight to preserve a Southern heritage for Maryland seems at times futile, Shane Long, a young Baltimorean and member of the SCV's Mechanized Cavalry, tells me that in his travels around the state he has met many natives who proudly know themselves to be Southerners. And Jim Dunbar says that it is elected officials who have presented problems for his organization, but he is not disheartened because the SCV is well-received everywhere by the people of Maryland. Can it be that there is hope for us? Maybe we're *not* completely Northernized—not yet.

CULTURE AND SOCIETY

Growing Old in the South

I was raised in a place where the family was the most cherished institution. Because of the societal pathologies spawned by cultural cleansing in Maryland and the larger South there is now an eroding of this most basic of social units and a growing acceptability of the abandonment of the young and old, the former to daycare, the latter to "homes" for the elderly. Feeling no shame in stealing money from taxpayers, families too readily send Maw Maw and Grand Pop to large Medicaid-subsidized nursing centers which charge exorbitant prices, prices inflated precisely because of the government's meddling in the free market. The children of the warehoused old folks make quick, perfunctory visits to these inmate wretches and beat a hasty retreat from the horrors of aging to the outside world where they can soothe themselves with the salve of materialism. As a creeping Northeastern-Left Coast secularism threatens the still-Christian South, as TV family values replace Southern family values, the Southern reverence for elders is waning.

Although a male friend of mine considers so much feminist drivel the belief that women become invisible as we age, I have to admit I sometimes feel a little spectral myself. As I become less philosophical about growing older, I understand better the drastic measures to which ladies go to hold on to youth and why LifeStyle Lift is doing such a booming business. And I sometimes think that worse than being invisible is having one's age noticed. I dread the day somebody pats me on the head and calls me feisty, or, God forbid, spry.

What is especially galling is the younger person's assumption that all of existence is nothing but the insignificant sliver of time during which he inspires and expires, his notion that the old were never young and are somehow less than human. In a very real sense aging is "payback" for the callousness of youth. And I think maybe God makes us suffer the indignities of the advanced years to teach us compassion and humility. Flannery O'Connor would say that turning into an old crone—something she was denied—is not as much a cross to bear as an opportunity to receive God's grace. But I still find myself rebellious towards God when it comes to maturing. I am essentially that same girl in the high school yearbook photograph, just wiser than she and better schooled in the female artifice that corrects nature's imperfections, and I am not going very gently into that good night. Also, as people are inclined to do, I am starting to look back to my heyday, wishing that I knew then what I know now, mooning over Gerry and the Pacemakers' greatest hits and pining for a decade to which only distance lends any charm. The reality is that, a National Honor Society scag, poor and unpopular among classmates, I was not all that happy then. No matter, the 1960s look better all the time compared to a future in a cold, progressive police state in which the mature are the subjects of contempt and socialist scheming.

Socialists hate old people; even old socialists hate old people. Long-in-the-tooth leftists, many apparently oblivious to their own need for a nip and a tuck and to the low snickering of that "eternal Footman," make fun of Tea Party geezers and warn the young not to listen to the outmoded, undemocratic ideas of the arthritic and crotchety. Even in its decline, the South remains the last Christian nation, a land where people are defined by more than age (or wealth), where they are less likely to be despised just for living.

I do not mean, however, to suggest that there was ever some perfect antediluvian Dixie where all classes behaved admirably always, and ladies did not fade from view simply because the bloom was off the rose. In the Old South, older women were expected to withdraw, to sit quietly—to be William Alexander Percy's "broad-bosomed lares and penates against the wall" looking on as the sweet-faced and beautiful waltzed around the ballroom. Old age came early in the Old South. Mary Chestnut, in recalling her arrival at the Kingsville, South Carolina railway station as the War of Secession was drawing to a close, reveals the plight of a woman of forty-three fending for herself in a land grown alien.

Maryland, My Maryland

Without fear I stepped off at Kingsville. My old Confederate silk, like most Confederate dresses, had seen better days, and I noticed that, like Oliver Wendell Holmes's famous "one-hoss shay," it had gone to pieces suddenly, and all over. It was literally in strips. I became painfully aware of my forlorn aspect when I asked the telegraph man the way to the hotel, and he was by no means respectful to me. I was, indeed, alone—an old and not too respectable-looking woman. It was my first appearance in the character, and I laughed aloud.[1]

The rude treatment that Mrs. Chestnut received from the telegraph operator and later at the hotel from "a very haughty and highly painted dame" was an indication that society was breaking down in the wartime South, that the scum was rising by degrees to the surface as Rose Greenhow noted in her memoirs. And the "bottom rail on top"—at least until the Southern aristocracy was reestablished after a fashion—it had no patience for an "old" woman in rags.

In this present era of Hydroxatone and Botox, a time when "they" say forty is the new thirty and forty-somethings are unapologetic for their adolescent and solipsistic outlook on life, Mary Chestnut, provided she did her Pilates and knew "what not to wear," at forty-three would still be considered young. But in the twenty-first century, when old age does finally overtake us no matter how fast we run from it, much more courage is required to face it than was required in Mary Chestnut's day, the aberrations of the War of Secession to the contrary notwithstanding. Growing old is unforgivable in a society desperately trying to forget that death is the great inevitability.

Often the subject of jokes ribald and cruel, old people are no longer the beneficiaries of the courtesy and morality that once offered a measure of protection to the weakest members of society. The young reject such anachronisms as courtesy, believing that the quaint values of gross-looking old hags and coots no longer apply, hence the downward spiral of culture and the destruction of polite social interaction, hence a nation-wide coarseness and barbarity made manifest as time goes on. Rather than the Christian charity of kin folk and neighbors, "senior citizens" (a Yankee term), as they make their way in the world, must rely on the kindness of "eldercare" workers and government regulators, if they decide to be kind. In an intact Southern society, decency and good manners, the latter the expression of the former, do not become obsolete, and bad manners are not thought of as some new (and liberating) phenomenon: They were in evidence when the first reeking hominoid slouched out of the swamp.

Because of the neopagan ruling class's push to allow fallen human nature full range, the aged have been robbed of their humanity. They are regarded as fungible and malleable; they are to be humored and managed and used to political advantage. Old men, however, are sometimes a problem because they are masculine and not as easily bullied as young bloodless and blubbering metrosexuals. Old women are seen by the socialist elite as foolish, bridge-playing or Branson-visiting nonentities who are to be resented for breathing on and on. Nevertheless they pander to their fears and pitch to them Marxist projects—Medicare, Medicaid and gun control—all for the purpose of keeping them "safe." But the only real safety for the "least of these" is to be found in a God-fearing family and local community and a well-oiled double-action revolver. And there is refuge still in the South, wherever true Southern culture thrives, not only for old ladies but for all those pot-throwing, soap-making hippies who flock to the highlands and other rural areas to escape the egalitarian, multicultural nightmares they have helped to create in the North with their liberal politics.

Two Murders

For many years I was associated with the St. Mary's County Historical Society, first serving as the organization's administrator, and, after leaving this paid position, volunteering as the assistant editor of the *Chronicles of St.*

Maryland, My Maryland

Mary's, the society's quarterly journal. While I was the administrator I was given an office in the Old Jail Museum, which happens to have figured into an horrific episode of the county's history.

Sitting in a corner of the front lawn of the courthouse in Leonardtown, the Old Jail was built in the mid-nineteenth century. At its entrance is a cannon brought to Maryland in the 1600s. When I was employed there, my office was downstairs in the area that at one time served as the sleeping quarters for the jailer and his family who lived right on the premises. The prisoners were housed upstairs in one of three cells: what were designated as the lady's and the men's cells, and, because there was racial segregation, a larger cell for black people.

In the early 1940s, the jail became miserably overcrowded. While the Patuxent River Naval Air Station was under construction, a great influx of transient workers increased the local population and the crime rate drastically. Prior to World War II, the jail had never been a very busy place except during prohibition when revenuers used it to detain those caught for making whiskey. Because St. Mary's County people saw nothing wrong with this time-honored custom and had a long-standing tradition of resisting the Federal Government's dictates, these prisoners were treated as guests by the jailer. They were allowed to leave the jail to play cards at the hotel on the town square or to play baseball, a very popular sport in the county. I found that visitors to the Old Jail always appreciated these anecdotes.

From my office on the first floor, I could see the courthouse with its white columns and beautifully tended grounds where weddings frequently were held. The wedding parties that gathered on the lawn were usually small, one ceremony as I recall attended only by the clerk of court and the bride and groom, both of whom wore denim. But at a more formal summer afternoon wedding, there were dozens of people dressed in brilliant colors, the scene reminding me of a Jonathan Green painting. It was almost unimaginable that on the same courthouse lawn in the 1880s, a lathered-up mob tried to hang a man named Benjamin Hance whose life was temporarily spared when a prominent local citizen living nearby told the lynchers to hang him elsewhere.

The murder that took place on that June night in 1887 was the climax to a series of events that set the stage for vigilantism and began with another murder in August 1886. Captain Robert R. Dixon, who was from Baltimore, was killed aboard the Mary J not by Hance but by a Charles County, Maryland man named Benjamin Biscoe, the son of an ex-slave.

Biscoe's erratic and suspicious behavior following the discovery of Captain Dixon's sloop near Leonardtown caught the attention of the sheriff, and not long after that, Dixon's body washed ashore across the river in Westmoreland County, Virginia. Biscoe was tried in Port Tobacco, Maryland because it was thought that he would not receive a fair trial in St. Mary's. He was found guilty, but the appeals process lasted until February 1888, and Biscoe was finally executed in April almost two years after the murder of Dixon.

But before he was hanged, another man, Hance, a Virginian, was taken from the jail and murdered by vigilantes for his attempted assault on a young woman. The lynching of Hance was a reaction on the part of a handful of men to the Freedman's Bureau's interference in the Biscoe case. Regardless of their motivations, they deprived Hance of the God-given right to a fair trial, having abducted and hanged him from a witch hazel tree beside a country road a few miles from Leonardtown. The rise in land where he was lynched is call Rip Gut Hill because of the defiling of his remains after the hanging.

There were one or two evenings that I worked overtime at the Old Jail, but I wasn't fond of staying there after dark. I often thought about Benjamin Hance and the terror he must have experienced in his last hours. I thought of his hearing the sound of the ax as the lynch mob chopped down first the wooden door to the jail and then the one to the large cell and dragged him out into the night. Those men murdered Benjamin Hance as sure as Biscoe murdered Dixon. Telling this story, to no political or sociological end, when I was conducting tours of the Old Jail, I seemed to make some visitors, most of them vacationers from out of state, uncomfortable, and a few made bitter comments about the backward locals and their treatment of minorities. But human beings, black or white, in their fallen condition, sometimes do terrible things. To paraphrase Aristotle, what happened, happened. History should neither mourn nor celebrate. It should simply witness.

Yankeefying Dixie

Contentious, red tape-loving Yankee newcomers are turning the South into the North not just because legions of them are moving here but because many Southerners are not really bothered by the cultural cleansing of their region. Concerned with little else than what is on TV and what Andrew Lytle called the "bric-a-brac" of the New South, they boil down that which defines the Southerner to pride in a college football team or the neighborhood all-you-can-eat franchise restaurant because unlike Jersey joints it serves "sweet tea" (a redundancy) or what passes for grits and greens. In the meantime, Yankees, with their Quisling toadies, are busy ridding the South of her "bad habits."

No one in the South wants to go North and fix things, but for some time now Northerners have been meddling below the Mason-Dixon. While the Yankee personality is comfortable with lots of complicated and codified limitations on personal freedom, Southerners are driven crazy by them. We prefer to let things work themselves out organically. We like rule making to be at a minimum. We don't thrive as the Yankees do on litigation and neighbor-against-neighbor feuds over every aspect of life. Southerners don't call Animal Control because the dog down the street is barking. Dogs bark. It is natural. Home Owner Associations also drive us up a wall. While HOAs are a Yankee dream come true, Southerners would rather not have a board of busybody control freaks telling us when and if we can fly a banner or flag or how many vehicles we may park in front of our house or in what kind of condition those vehicles have to be. Yankees want a perfect world; Southerners don't look for one or try to impose one on others.

And a perfect world to a Northerner is by definition a smokeless one. In Maryland, once a top tobacco-producing state, carpetbaggers for decades have been crusading against the sot weed hoping eventually to outlaw it all together. Illustrative of what tyrannical people Yankees are is an incident that took place a few years ago at a hospital in my home county. Attempting to escape from the psychiatric ward, an eccentric little woman with a quaint Southern Maryland name only made it as far as the main lobby when a carpetbagger rent-a-cop stopped her as she was heading for the door. He seemed less focused, however, on her breaking out than on the unlit cigarette in her mouth. She had made no attempt to light it, had no matches or lighter in her hands, but the security guard ordered the lady to remove the cigarette in spite of this. Had she walked around with unlit Marlboros sticking out of both her ears and her mouth, no one had the right to demand she remove them because she wasn't breaking the law. The guard, of course, wasn't thinking about legality; he just wanted to push someone around worked up as he was in his Pavlovian response to the sight of a cigarette. (Yankees have an enormous need for absolute control: Since 2003 in New York City, the presence of an ashtray, even if it holds "paper clips or M & M's," is in violation of the city's anti-smoking laws.[1])

That hospital for which he worked has as its director a New York woman who has removed from the walls of the cafeteria and other areas some particularly well-done photos of old tobacco barns. They were removed because of the complaint of one nurse, a Northerner, who was possessed of the Yankee's characteristic pushiness and abhorrence of anything related to tobacco.

Swamped as well with expatriate Yankees, one of whom has recently become governor of the commonwealth, Virginia has also joined the ranks of those states with more stringent anti-smoking laws. As the carpetbaggers continue to reform the Upper South and as the cigarette smoke clears over the Old Dominion and Maryland, some of us are, nevertheless, choking on the foul air of repression.

Redneck Girls and Southern Belles

I'm a redneck woman,
And I ain't no high class broad.
I'm just a product of my raisin'.
I say "hey y'all" and "yee haw."
I keep my Christmas lights on on my front porch all year long,
And I know all the words to every Charlie Daniels song.
—John Rich and Gretchen Wilson

I like Gretchen Wilson's Grammy-award winning hit "Redneck Woman." I like rednecks; they are an integral part of Southern society. But something about "RW" really disturbs me, and it isn't that it is tacky though it is. The problem is that the song promotes Southern stereotypes when it assumes that, on one hand, there are "high class broads" (read Yankees) and, on the other hand, women who say "hey y'all," the latter being lower class. The implication is that Southern speech and Southern culture are inferior to Northern. But this is not true.

Some Southerners, especially the young, while taking pride in their Southern ways, still believe the myth that Yankees are erudite and well bred. To the contrary, most Northerners are poorly educated—technical training is not education. In the North (and in the occupied South), where class is largely a matter of money, riffraff rise to the top. And though the South has traditionally drawn its strength from both its earth and realm—the former more faithfully preserving the old speech which might have been lost to us forever—the earthiest elements are better consigned to the bottom rungs of the social ladder even if they have "pockets full of gold."

Though all Southerners have some things in common— a love of Southern cuisine and pickup trucks, a love of hunting and, until Yankees ruined it, stock car racing—there are distinctions among them. At the top are the Southern aristoi, who have traditionally been the descendants of the old planter society; refined and well read, they, in theory, are born to leadership. The Southern gentry class has not disappeared all together, but they are, however, less influential, and their children and grandchildren, talking and acting "Yankee," are virtually indistinguishable from Northerners. The Southern aristocrat not being defined by money or property until more recent times, it is not so surprising that one example of this class in the 1950s worked as a clerk in a general store in Southern Maryland. A classical scholar and graduate of Loyola College, when he wasn't waiting on customers, he would read his Virgil and Thucydides. The farmer and waterman par occasion who spoke three languages fluently and who was known to wear gum boots and sit in his kitchen at four a.m. shucking oysters for fritters, the college graduate who would listen to *Murder in the Cathedral* on tapes as he stripped tobacco in the barn, the country doctors whose libraries included works by Josephus and Xenophon all represented the best of Southern society.

Confirming Yankee presuppositions about the South, a beer-swilling, pot-bellied mobile home dweller scratching and cussing—the Southerner you typically find on daytime and reality television—has become the personification of the Southland replacing that cultured store clerk, that T.S. Elliot-loving tobacco stripper, those gentlemen physicians and all those Southern, bourbon-sipping polymaths who used to sit on summer porches with friends listening to whippoorwills and talking about history and politics late into sticky nights. The South, at least it seems, is no longer the land of Donald Davidson and William Faulkner but of Uncle Si and Honey Boo Boo. (If the producers of *Duck Dynasty* would leave out the unnecessary raunchiness, I would be a fan of the show because it is otherwise entertaining and politically incorrect—and I love Miss Kay and Phil—but as it stands now the scatological humor is injurious to the South's dignity and image. I won't comment further on Honey Boo Boo.)

Well-mannered but not as genteel as the gentry, plain folks—that is, good old boys and girls—make up the Southern middle class. They live in the country, suburban subdivisions, even the city; they are the heart and soul of their region. Just below plain folks are the rednecks—the line between the two classes is not sharply drawn. Usually associated with the rural South though they can be found in urban areas, rednecks are rough around the edges but essentially decent people even if they have scrapes with the law from time to time. Hard-working, family-loving, hard-drinking—unless he's washed in the blood—the redneck is as close to being a free man as this brave new world will allow.

At the lowest rung of Southern society are welfare-dependent trash who are just plain rough (the pot-bellied beer swillers may fall into this category but not necessarily). Trash should never be entrusted with authority, because they see it as a tool for revenge. Self-assured all out of proportion to their abilities, they are not very polite although far more courteous than most Northerners; they are often violent and mistreat women and children. Frequently settling family matters by calling the police, they are the authors of their own misery given to self-pity and resentment towards their betters.

Carpetbaggers have a difficult time distinguishing Southern gentry and good old boys from rednecks, rednecks from trash. But Southern people have no such problem. The trashy class of Southern society may be growing as the South degenerates, but there are still those of an aristocratic bearing, self-disciplined and moral, who have assumed leadership roles, who are striving for a Southern renaissance. Among them is the much-maligned Southern lady, a personality who has always transcended class. Reduced by outsiders to a comic figure, witless and deceitful, she is none of those things and is very aware that her world and her family are threatened. She knows how to shoot a gun so it is a mistake to identify her as prey. She is gracious even when she feels like cursing; cheerful when she doesn't want to be. She doesn't leave her Christmas lights on all year round as the redneck woman does; she may prefer Debussy to Charlie Daniels, but she is proud to be Southern, and she says "y'all." And she would much rather live next door to Redneck Woman than trash or Yankees.

Joyce Bennett

Beware That Which You Don't Understand

It is small wonder that some people in the South have tried to "secede" from their own region considering that many of them have come to accept as truth the propagandizing of South-hating Northern bigots. In a 2002 commentary for the *St. Petersburg Times*, Bill Maxwell asks, "Exactly who are Southerners? Are they still benighted, gravy-slopping rednecks who would rather fish than work?"[1] The implication here is that though once contemptible, uncouth and lazy, Southerners might possibly be making a little "progress." As the ancient Greeks, however, Southern people understand the value of a life that balances industry with a constructive leisure. Yankees are Romans—overly precise and manic. As for the slopping of gravy, Northerners are the ones with the bad table manners, not Southerners.

Maxwell says that he is the son of migrant farmers, a Southerner who "rediscovered" the South after "travels through rural Georgia, the Carolinas and Virginia," a telling admission on the part of a Floridian. He seems to have affection for the Southland but still takes the obligatory potshots at it (obligatory in the sense that the journalist who doesn't at least mention the "sins" of the South will not be published in a big city newspaper). Quoting a few stereotype re-enforcers who may or may not be authentic Southerners themselves, Maxwell works in the always necessary reminder that the South has a "special view" of American history and "unlike any other area, a lasting shame."

If by "special view" he means an insistence on the truth about history, Maxwell is correct. But he is wrong in suggesting that Southerners alone have something to live down: New England, Britain and France also profited from the slave trade. But their involvement in it will be conveniently forgotten; the South will never be forgiven for slavery.

Maxwell pokes fun at "his" Dixie with the somewhat pointless jest that "you have to be smart and have a sense of humor if you are born and raised in a place that is home to Elvis...Delta blues, grits, boiled peanuts and the seersucker suit." By smart, does he mean "hip" enough to rise above such regrettable Southern symbols? Or does he mean sufficiently intelligent to have deep insights into the cultural "aberrations" that give rise to boiled peanuts? And would Maxwell disagree that an appreciation of the blues requires a sense of the aesthetic? He seems to have overlooked the fact that the South is as much a land of magnificent neoclassical architecture, gracious social customs, gifted and wonderfully eccentric writers and unequaled cuisine as it is of its folksier aspects, as delightful as they are.

While Southern people do find, as Maxwell says, ironies in everyday things, expressing them as only they can with their facility for and love of language, there is nothing particularly humorous about grits. Though Elvis's garish costumes were comical, he could sing. And seersucker is no joke either: It is attractive and practical for hot, humid weather. Hopefully, it will make a comeback.

With the condescension of a Yankee-accommodating scalawag, Maxwell writes that "clever Southerners know how to cultivate and maintain the region's beloved coarse image." But how can a people who place the highest premium on dignified and courteous behavior be "coarse"? This is purely an invention of the defamer of the South and the self-loathing Southerner who allows Northeast and West Coast types to do his thinking for him. Maxwell may be confusing coarseness with homeyness and the polite rusticity that Southerners love to rub in the face of the ever-pretentious and materialistic Yankee, but coarseness, the norm elsewhere, is the exception in the South: Good manners live in the humblest of homes below the Mason-Dixon.

After dispensing with the perfunctory insults to the South, Maxwell, who actually seems to have affection for his own people, settles down to a more serious discussion of the Southern personality properly asserting that "most Southerners" consider the Yankee's rapid speech rude and a tool of the aggressor. But they are not afraid of the Northerner as "cultural observer" Julia Reed, quoted by Maxwell, suggests. Reed believes that the "deep-dyed fear that lives in the heart of every Southerner... is that a Yankee is putting us down." But putting down Southerners is the stock and trade of the Northerner, who, as Maxwell notes, considers our speech a sure sign of mental or educational deficiency. Southerners, in reality, do not fear Yankee ridicule. What we fear mostly is our reaction to the aggression and ignorance of the Yankee. Failing to understand the habit of courtesy, Northerners have no idea how angry a Southerner may be or how much strength of will is required to remain civil when he wants to smack the smugness off a Northern face. Southerners are socialized to be nice even if it kills us. And it often does. But we are not afraid of Yankees or what they might think or say; we are afraid only of ourselves.

The Country Girl

(This essay appeared in the May 2013 issue of *Chronicles: A Magazine of American Culture* published by The Rockford Institute, Rockford, Illinois.)

The fall the Orioles won their first World Series, I was rooming off-campus with three other Towson State College freshmen in a three-story house on Evesham Avenue. The Baltimore of the mid-1960's was not as much ashamed of its heritage as unschooled in it, most Baltimoreans not knowing— or caring—that, under the shade of the trees [in Wyman Park], Jackson and Lee in "unwearying bronze" still met on the eve of Chancellorsville. By that time F. Scott Fitzgerald's "civilized and gay...rotted and polite" old port was well on its way to morphing into Philadelphia. As a product of the tobacco culture of Southern Maryland, I was homesick but still caught up in the novelty of living in a working-class urban neighborhood and thrilled by some aspects of the city, unsuspecting of its evils until almost too late.

Usually, I would ride the bus to classes, but I remember a few winter mornings when a couple of us would carpool with a fellow student who would swing by Evesham before sunrise on his way to the college. Although his VW Bug had no heater, it did have a radio, and, despite the cold, my low spirits would lift as I listened to the Four Tops and the Rolling Stones on WCAO. Lonesomeness and the feeling of being out of my element were almost gone by the time we saw the campus and the lights of the dining hall with their promise of hot coffee and, to me, delicious—if greasy—institutional food prepared by fat cafeteria women. The elder of only two daughters in a family of eight children, I found not having to cook for others or to wash dishes an unimaginable luxury. When the pack wasn't empty there was also the after-breakfast Winston to enjoy—and we could smoke practically anywhere on campus in those days.

In the afternoons, I always took the bus home. The house where I roomed was owned by a John S__, a beatnik and a self-styled abstract artist. While his wife seemed, oddly enough, very middle-class, John, in my mind, was the epitome of nonconformity and sophistication. Decades later of course I know that he was a cliché, and so were those ugly modern paintings of his that hung on the walls of the second-floor apartment we girls rented, but back then I was impressed with him even if I felt uncomfortably country in his presence. Nervous and tongue-tied, I never knew what to say to him.

One of my roommates was descended from old Maryland families, but because she had lived all her life in the *nouveau venu*-corrupted suburbs of D.C., she spoke with an appreciably Northern accent. Dressed in the high fashion of the day—I coveted her Bass Weejuns and suede jacket—she was confident, socially poised, and was asked to Naval Academy dances. The others included a classmate from high school (a good-natured military brat but not a true native) and Barbara Jean, from Salisbury, who had an Eastern Shore accent so thick you could have cut it with a knife. The way she had of speaking, which was more standard Southern and more pronounced than my own tidewater accent, was a subject of ridicule: The girl from suburbia and that goateed landlord of ours had nothing but contempt for it and for Barbara Jean. Not realizing that their snobbery was rooted in ignorance, I didn't question their judgment on what was and was not correct speech.

Having been born and raised in outlying unreconstructed Maryland, Barbara Jean was undoubtedly countrified, but I was as well, though I pretended otherwise. And, late one night on Evesham Avenue, with the ringing of the third-story doorbell, that lack of guile we had in common, in spite of my putting on airs, almost proved our undoing. Even though I knew that each floor of the house had its own distinctive "buzzer," awakened from a deep sleep, I, nevertheless, went downstairs to the foyer without thinking that our second-story bell had not rung, that no one lived above our apartment that semester, and that no one had any business calling at midnight anyway. I opened the door, and standing in front of me was a man. A dockworker or a millhand type, he was a brutish hulk with a crew cut.

I will never forget the question he asked me: "How many of you are up there?"

As if I were hypnotized, I politely responded, "Four."

He replied, "Too many."

Fully awake by this time, I had the presence of mind to close and secure the door. In retrospect, I was only able to do this because he had decided to leave us alone.

I realized then that my lack of caution had exposed my friends and me to God knows what that night. Shaken and mortified, I faced my roommates upstairs. I was relieved, however, to hear Barbara Jean speak up to say that a few days before the incident, a man who matched my description of the would-be intruder had struck up a conversation with her at the corner drugstore. Unduly flattered, the unattractive and big-boned Barbara Jean had volunteered too much information about herself to this stranger. I joined the others in chiding her, happy to have a scapegoat and to divert attention from the fact that I too had not developed the city dweller's habit of wariness. City people knew instinctively that, in the dead of night, it wasn't wise to unbolt a lock without first finding out who was on the other side of it. But Barbara Jean, I rationalized, was the more culpable because she had inadvertently invited the hulk to come calling. I didn't stand by the down-home, neighborly but shy, Southern-talking young woman, but chose instead to join those who blamed her—and, thank goodness, not me—for that midnight encounter with the devil.

Not long ago, from my Western Shore home, I discovered that I could tune in the faint signal of an AM radio station broadcasting from across the

Chesapeake Bay. Its rustic, locally produced ads for Ronnie's Garage and other area merchants afforded me the opportunity to hear Barbara Jean's pretty Eastern Shore accent again. I wish I could go back to those college days and defend her trusting ways to my roommates and explain that I had opened the door to danger that night because I, too, was an innocent Southern girl making my way in the brave new Baltimore.

On Courtesy

One day in the town where I was born, I met a trio of twenty-somethings walking along side by side. They never looked at me. Unseeing, they just marched dead ahead towards me. Courtesy dictates that in tight places we go to the right to accommodate the people we are meeting, but, never having acknowledged my existence, these zombies would have stumbled right over me had I not stepped onto the grass to avoid a collision. Making room for others on sidewalks or on the highway or in store aisles is one of those small acts of kindness that contribute to a civilized society. But where I live Southern civility is in its death throes.

Contrary to what Yankees believe, good manners require tremendous strength; bad manners are a sign of weakness. Courteous behavior is not complicated, and if the habit of courtesy is deeply ingrained, it will not fail. A beautiful example, I think, of what constitutes proper Southern manners is this: Many years ago, a well-respected lady in my county, who was dying at home, learned one morning that her doctor would be making a house call. She forced herself to get out of her death bed, dressed, put on jewelry and perfume so that she could go downstairs to receive him properly in the living room. Later that same day she died. Southerners wise enough to have resisted Yankeefying influences and those among us who have emerged from our cultural stupor and now regret our former affectation of Northern behavior, hold firmly to the belief that there is never an excuse for a lack of courtesy.

A carpetbagger woman objecting to my characterization of Yankees as ill mannered, once insisted that she was polite—most of the time. She proved my point: Southerners consistently demonstrate good manners even when it is inconvenient or difficult to do so.

Yankees and Southerners especially differ on acceptable behavior related to driving. The real Southerner is not as susceptible to road rage as the Yankee, the latter's eyes bulging, his mouth foaming as he rides the bumpers of vehicles the operators of which have the nerve to obey the speed limit or to travel only a few miles an hour faster than the law allows. Not only do Southerners not tailgate, we do not honk at funeral processions, but, instead, late for appointments or not, pull over to the side of the road when meeting them saying some prayers for the repose of the soul of the deceased (at one time people would stand outside their cars and pray). Southerners also pull off the road when meeting or being followed by an ambulance or fire truck. And we drive in our own lane on a country road particularly when going up hills and around curves. Further, we do not pass a left-turning vehicle by driving on the shoulder of the road. Yankees do this. It is becoming increasingly dangerous to navigate the highways carpetbaggers have turned into war zones.

What is most disturbing to me is the general impression that other Southerners have of my much-changed community now that it is home to so many Northerners. A lady from farther South was visiting a carpetbagger who had moved to our area because of her husband's defense-related employment. The Southerner was amazed at the lack of friendliness in the check-out lines at a supermarket not far from the Navy base that dominates our economy and remarked to her carpetbagger hostess that where she was from people talked to each other and were nicer, the Yankee slightly amused and in agreement that things were different "in the South." But the Southern visitor and the carpetbagger were in the South, the South that the carpetbagger and others like her have destroyed or almost destroyed.

The presence of the Navy and other factors have transformed my county into one of the wealthiest in the U.S., but we now suffer from spiritual and cultural impoverishment. At another local grocery store, I witnessed one of the most outrageous instances of solipsism and bad manners yet. While

Maryland, My Maryland

I was at the "deli" (a Yankee concept), I noticed just ahead of me in line a young "lady" in her teens and her mother. The mother, who had a Northern accent, was a bit more polished, but the daughter was sighing loudly at having to wait her turn with the rest of us, and, at one point, sat her denim short-short-clad derrière on the deli counter because she didn't feel like standing. Her mother asked her to get down but not immediately. What kind of raising did this wild killdee have that would have led her to believe she could do this in the first place?

I have also found, not surprisingly, plenty of rudeness at the big box stores catering to newcomers in our area. The hordes at Walmart will run you over with shopping carts if you are not careful. Much of Walmart merchandise is made in China so I don't really want to shop there anyway, and I usually don't. I like to shop at country stores, dollar stores, thrift shops and the like because the customers and clerks are still very polite. These are places Yankee transplants don't normally frequent. At our local Penney's and Belk's the sales clerks are also amiable; it is the customers there who are the rude ones. Even at Christmas time—especially at Christmas time— I find most shoppers are on their worst behavior. While the mention of Christ is strictly forbidden in public schools at this holiest time of year, the Christless, Godless graduates of these federal indoctrination centers are "acting out" in the market place. They are f-bomb-dropping vandals storming the gates and ransacking stores leaving clothing and merchandise strewn all over. I should thank God I guess that in our immediate area it is not necessary—not yet—for store managers to call out the riot police on Black Friday.

I remember a liberal's calling in to a radio talk show to remark that the vile behavior of the Occupy Wall Street protesters was an expression of youthful exuberance and fresh new modern attitudes. But there is nothing fresh or new about degeneracy. In fact, mankind's fallen condition and tendency towards the barbarous are the reasons for the birth of Christ. It is our flawed nature—and I say this as a former liberal and agnostic—that requires us to seek Christ's redemption. If Christ did not compel us to be charitable towards others even when life is not going our way, we could be as rude as we wished. If He did not compel us to hold the door for those who follow us into Penney's, we could just let it slam in their faces. If Christ did not compel us to pick up off a department store floor a Liz Claiborne sweater that has fallen off a hanger, we could walk away and leave it there. We wouldn't be bothered with keeping the store neater, or saving time and effort for hard-working employees or preventing someone else's expensive item from becoming soiled. And without the mandates from Christ what is to stop us, gimlet-eyed and set-jawed, as we trample to death another shopper who dares get between us and that hundred dollar-flat screen TV? But God knows when the sparrow falls; He takes note of what we do, our seemingly unexciting and small charitable acts. He is with us even at the mall.

The Fall of the House of Chaptico

Born in New England—his actor parents touring there at the time—Edgar Allan Poe was orphaned as a very small child and was taken in by John Allan who raised him in Richmond where Poe was to reside off and on over the years. He also lived, sometimes under wretched circumstances, in Boston, New York, Philadelphia, Charleston and other cities, but his father's people were Baltimoreans, though relative latecomers by Maryland standards. By blood, then, as well as by breeding, the restless Poe was a Southerner, his familial ties to Baltimore, where he lies buried today, making him at the very least as much a Marylander as a Virginian. Further, there is a theory—mostly of my own devising—that a tragedy in a tiny village in Southern Maryland inspired one of his tales.

In *A Southern Treasury of Life and Literature,* which includes examples from the works of several Marylanders, Stark Young defends Poe against a Northern literary establishment that favored Yankee Anglo-mimics over Southern writers who were considered "at best roughly humorous or folksy." With the unexpected "endorsement of Europe," Young writes, Poe, who had been "recognized but always with uncertainty and often with apology," eventually proved to have had "more life in art...than a hundred Longfellows, Bryants, and Whittiers lumped together."[1]

In his introduction to *The Complete Tales and Poems of Edgar Allan Poe*, an anthology published in 1938, Hervey Allen deplores the fact that for many years Poe's literary legacy was preserved only in "obscure...female and piffling" magazines and other less-than-respectable publications.

> *The aftermath of Poe's death was a long and intricate story full of the sound and fury of a controversy about the nature of the man's personality, his loves and misfortunes, and for years it was a tale told by idiots, male and female, in which incredible oceans of slushy sentimentality, bathos and wishy-washy hysteria broke in waves of froth over the submerged rocks of fact.*[2]

A "slushy sentimentality" sometimes coloring my own perspectives on Poe, I continue to hope for proof of a connection between his *Fall of the House of Usher* and something that took place in the 1800s in Chaptico, Maryland, an old town just five minutes from my home in St. Mary's County.

A trusted friend told me that when he was in the Coast Guard in the very early 1960s, while sitting in the waiting room of a military office, he saw among the magazines on a coffee table an auction house brochure advertising letters written to Poe from by an in-law in Chaptico (or written by him to the in-law; my friend cannot recall exactly). It is possible that this correspondence be counterfeit even considering that Chaptico isn't the type of location that would immediately spring to mind if someone were engaged in deception of this sort. For what it is worth, my mother recalls that in the early 1930s as a young girl attending Hickory Hills, a one-room school house, she heard her teacher, Miss Annie, speak of Poe's having visited Chaptico, a place the history and legends of which are equally interesting.

When the British occupied the town during the War of 1812, they behaved so abominably that local authorities appealed to President Madison for help—appealed in vain as he responded that he had no troops to spare to defend every Southern Maryland farmer's turnip patch. During the War of Secession, the Yankees were the occupiers of Chaptico, nonetheless a hub of Southern underground activities and a haven for Confederate soldiers seeking refuge. Local folklorists celebrate the heroism of Catharine Hayden, who was to become known all over the South as the Angel of Chaptico, because this young epileptic, risking execution by the Yankees at Point Lookout, smuggled medicines and food to convalescing Confederates hiding out in the area. On December 26, 1872, she died from burns sustained on Christmas Day when suffering a seizure she fell into a blazing hearth.

Just outside Chaptico proper is the home of Richard Thomas Zarvona, the famous—or infamous, the Yankee would say—French Lady who with just a few men captured the Union vessel the St. Nicholas. Thomas, after whom my United Daughters of the Confederacy chapter is named, was wiry, slender and not very tall from all reports. He disguised himself as a woman and, speaking French and flirting, beguiled and distracted the passengers and Yankee crew. Suddenly he and those who had come aboard with him took out their pistols and commandeered the ship, delivering it into the hands of the Confederates.

Folklore says that Chaptico served as a base camp for Yankee troops pursuing John Wilkes Booth. Union soldiers set up their headquarters at a crossroads inn, and it was from there that they spread out searching for Lincoln's assassin. The inn, which later served as a general store, is no longer standing, razed to make way for a liquor- and lottery ticket-selling Citgo station. Not far from the Citgo is Chaptico Market which is country and friendly and famous for its fried chicken and stuffed ham.

Chaptico was as late as 1935 a busy port where lighterage and steamboats anchored taking on cargo and passengers en route to Baltimore. It is believed that Gristis Venture, an ancient home, once stood overlooking Chaptico Bay, a deep waterway into which stilted tobacco warehouses projected, now only a quiet marsh, having silted in over the years.

According to some St. Mary's County people, though there are variations on the legend, which differs from Poe's tale in many respects,

Gristis Venture was the home of a prosperous planter with many slaves. He lived there with his wife who suffered from a terrible condition that left her disfigured except for her hands which remained unravished by the disease. Because of the pride she took in this last vestige of her youth and beauty, her husband bought her many expensive rings. As a consequence of all of this she would spend hours admiring her hands.

When the lady's maid one day came to the master to report her mistress had passed away, he buried his wife who was still wearing her rings in the graveyard at Christ Church. That evening after her funeral two watermen from Virginia were drinking in the village and heard about her death and about her jewelry. They, it is said, in their drunken state, defiled her grave. Unable to remove the rings from the "body," they started cutting off a finger with a knife. The woman, who had been buried prematurely, awoke at this point, scaring off the would-be grave robbers. Struggling up the hill to Gristis Venture, she appeared at her own front door, her white shroud soaked in blood from the mutilation of her hand. On answering the door and seeing the horrible sight at his threshold, her husband, who had been drinking, passed out knocking her down as he fell and dropping the lighted candle in his hand. This ignited the drapery and set the house on fire and both the man and woman perished as it burned to the ground. Today only a crumbling brick cellar overgrown with honeysuckle and dewberry vines remains of what is thought to have been that mansion.

The name Gristis Venture does not appear in county debt books or rent rolls, but there is an entry for a Gristy's Venture in Chaptico. I think that they are one and the same. Regardless, the similarities between the Gristis Venture tale and *Fall of the House of Usher* are easily dismissed, and in the light of such sketchy evidence should be dismissed, by scholars and researchers. If located, the missing letters would prove at least a Poe-Chaptico association. In my heart I think there was one. But then maybe I am just giving in to a little "fact-drowning bathos" of my own.

Joyce Bennett

Maryland in the Movies

Because of the media's portrayal of our state as the nondescript rust belt twin of New Jersey, Marylanders are rarely thought of as fox-hunting, julep-making "rebels" anymore but rather as amorphous Mid-Atlantic types or loud, hand-gesturing Theresa Caputos. Over the years, TV shows such as *Jerry Seinfeld*, which featured the very Northeastern character Elaine from Baltimore, have contributed to the stereotyping of Marylanders as Yankees. And though Maryland is the setting for a surprising number of movies today, very little of our culture comes through on the screen. There is more to us than the Birds and blue crabs. Old Hollywood was as leftist as New Hollywood, but the creators of classic cinema were at least educated in history, culture and regional distinctions.

A New York nightclubbing Southerner, having just informed the Zachary Scott character in *One Last Fling* that she had never before been "up North," is irritated by his asking if she had ever been to Maryland. She responds crossly in a painfully theatrical drawl that she had just said that she'd not visited the North before, a line that was intended to elicit laughter from 1949 moviegoers: The girl was "so Southern" she thought Maryland was Northern, a joke that would be lost on today's audiences.

The Great Lie confuses the Upper with the Lower South and the twentieth with the nineteenth century. In this 1941 production starring Bette Davis as a not-so-believable "modern' Maryland belle, there is a lot of anachronistic singing in the quarters and on the veranda and, "Lawsy yes," there is even a Mammy character played by Hattie McDaniel. Mary Astor plays the "high-tone New York lady" whose personality is as cold as the icy urban world in which she lives, Bette Davis the warm, feminine country girl who treats her servants kindly, sips on mint juleps and tolerates her pack of rabbit dogs as they lounge all over the big house even on the chintz-covered sofas. And on her old plantation, the Deep South variety of Spanish moss incongruously hangs in great profusion from ancient trees. But while kudzu, magnolias and cypress all can be found in Maryland, the state's Spanish moss is not the same type as that seen farther down in Dixie and is confined to a very small area of the Eastern Shore. Silly as it is, *The Great Lie* reveals that in the 1940s people would not have mistaken Maryland for Maine as they do today.

Though it takes some liberties with history, *The Prisoner of Shark Island*, which tells the story of Dr. Samuel Mudd, portrays the Yankees as villainous, the Marylanders as Southern. The musical score says it all in the movie *Gone With the Wind*. In one scene, at a bazaar held to raise money for the war effort, soldiers and their sweethearts, euphoric with high hopes for the Confederacy, are serenaded with a small orchestra's rendition of "Maryland! My Maryland!" Later in the movie, it is heard again as a dirge as the camera pans out for a wide view of bloodied and dying men as far as the eye can see.

Twenty-five years after the making of *Gone with the Wind*, Alfred Hitchcock's absurd film *Marnie* takes a stab at geographical and cultural authenticity. Hitchcock's heroine, played by Tippi Hedren, is from Baltimore, and while she speaks a bland American English, her mother's is Southern, actually a poorly rendered Appalachian. Hitchcock might have intended this character to be someone descended from the West Virginians who over the years have come to Baltimore for work. Nevertheless, Baltimore in this movie is clearly if bizarrely interpreted as Southern.

In the film adaptation of Edna Ferber's *Giant* the heroine is also a Marylander, not the Virginian of the novel. The movie contrasts life in the Old Line State's rolling, green hunt country with that of the flat and windy Texas plains, the almost effete older South with the more robust cowpoke South. Unfortunately Elizabeth Taylor's Leslie, who initially swoons at wild and woolly Western doings, in spite of her ladylike mannerisms turns out to be a strident feminist-egalitarian. In this respect the movie is true to the novel.

The liberal propaganda of Old Hollywood was in many ways far more insidious than anything the undisciplined talents of Tinsel Town today have dreamed up. The progressive message expressed through variations on the class-struggle theme is more effectively delivered with good plots, pleasant hometown settings and wholesome, well-scrubbed characters: Myrna Loy and Fredric March were such elegant leftists.

Joyce Bennett

Those old films in spite of their Marxist evangelizing were usually well-made, absorbing entertainment. Current cinema, though technologically marvelous, is obnoxiously preachy, and those of us with reasonable intelligence who resent transparent, poorly scripted attempts to brainwash us and who are put off by revisionist history, find them almost impossible to watch. This is why Robert Redford's *The Conspirator* comes as such a surprise. One explanation for the arch-liberal Redford's unexpectedly honest treatment of the judicial murder of Mary Surratt could be that he finds what happened to her useful as he advances the woman-as-victim myth and at the same time shines the light on evil Republicans (and they were evil). To give the devil his due, however, Redford has dared to tell the truth about Marylanders in the grip of Yankee tyranny during the great "Civil War."

Give Me That Old-Time Religion

(This essay appeared in the July 2010 issue of *Chronicles: A Magazine of American Culture* published by The Rockford Institute, Rockford, Illinois. Voter surveys can be found on the Maryland Catholic Conference's website at www.mdcathcon.org/marylandgovernment.)

In my 1950's childhood, boys and men, hair slicked down with tonic, girls and ladies in mantillas and hats primly veiled with mesh worshiped at small country churches against which lapped the green and white fields of late-summer tobacco. On Easter Sundays, prissy and full of ourselves on such a special occasion, my sister and I wore brand-new gloves and pastel dresses ballooned and swishy with crinoline and too proudly showed off our ribbon-and artificial-fruit-festooned bonnets. Descended from Maryland's earliest settlers, we were those rare birds—Catholics of English extraction. After four long decades, I was finally brought to a tearful reconciliation with my ancestral faith in spite of misgivings about the Marxist leanings of modern churchmen. And there is still for me sometimes on the Sabbath a temptation to drive over to the Southern Baptist services, because I am much more comfortable with the Baptists than with the wan contemporary Catholics I find at Mass these days (although the Baptist Church, according to Flannery O'Connor, is maybe a little too respectable for the real Catholic, who was, she insisted, not as far from her lunatic fundamentalist prophets as some of us might think).

I know that my criticisms of the present-day Church will be viewed by some as the crabbed grousings of just another rosary-praying Jansenist longing for the good old days. I have no illusions, however, about human shortcomings, and I understand that there were wrongdoers—even monsters—among the laity and clergy "way back when." But the Mystical Body endures despite Catholic hypocrites and sinners and despite the many who hate Catholicism not for what it is as much as for what it is not, to paraphrase Archbishop Fulton Sheen. Unfortunately, to accommodate those who are discomfited by "medieval" notions of sin and redemption, Catholicism in America is morphing most conveniently into Reverend Leroy's Church of What's Happenin' Now.

And a progressive Catholic hierarchy champions pet liberal causes, not the least of which is the "plight" of the immigrant. In a joint statement, the archbishops of Washington, D.C., and Baltimore, Donald Wuerl and Edwin F. O'Brien, droning on about the "dignity" of "persons" and comparing the undocumented to those "most precious migrants" Joseph, Mary, and Jesus, urge that Catholics not be distracted by mere "questions of legality." They do concede that "sovereign nations have the right to control their borders" but only "provided...regulations promote the common good of our universal human family," whatever that might mean. No matter how nuanced their rhetoric, I believe Catholic officials could not care less about stemming the tide of illegal immigration. When America collapses economically and socially, however, who then will bankroll Catholic Charities? The left-wingers at the chancelleries fail to make the distinction between a hateful xenophobia and a healthy interest in preserving the integrity of a nation's boundaries, as they similarly fail to delineate with real clarity unjust and just war.

Designed to stifle dissent, gratuitous charges of racism from the religious or secular left will not silence some of us. America has no obligation to commit national suicide in the name of brotherhood. (I do have to wonder if parish priests would be quite as inclined to provide church-basement asylum to undocumented Unitarians as they are to hide out illegal Catholics.) The U.S. bishops' view that everyone in the world should be allowed to move to America—and why not to Vatican City?—is a manifestation of collegiate sentimentality, not Christian love, which is reason itself. I know what Jesus would do: He would, with courteous resolve, send the *ilícito* ones packing.

Even if Church leaders could make a case for open borders, feel-good big-government largesse, and forced charity, there is no way around the abortion issue for those who call themselves Catholic. While a woman who believes she has a "right to choose" is perfectly free to reject Catholicism, she has no right to demand that the Church bend to her will, genuflect to her little gods. But Catholic leaders, it seems, are only halfheartedly defending the most vulnerable among us. Just before the 2006 elections, the Maryland Catholic Conference shockingly implied that a Church-friendly Maryland General Assembly candidate need only support safer abortion clinics, parental notification before underage girls abort babies (or take "morning-after" pills), and better data collection regarding the number of abortions performed. While correctly objecting to "the asexual creation of human embryos through cloning," the MCC did not condemn abortion outright, though it did in very clear terms call for the abolition of capital punishment.

An MCC 2008 survey sought to identify those congressional candidates who agreed that "Federal Policy should...restrict the use of taxpayer funds for abortion" and that "Federal agencies and states that receive federal funds should not discriminate against health care providers who do not perform or participate in abortions." The candidates, however, were not polled on the question of outlawing abortion. Why not?

Because Catholic officialdom offers only uneven and tepid defense of the unborn, come election day too many little old Church ladies who travel by the busload each spring to march on D.C. for the right to life mindlessly cast their ballots for pro-choice candidates. There is no point in suggesting to them that their politics are vile and not in keeping with an observance of the Fifth Commandment. They will not listen—at least not to just anyone. They might, however, heed a justifiably exercised clergy and prelacy.

Parish priests can plant little white crosses in the ground till Hell freezes over, but they will not reach the Catholics who—through ignorance or habit or defiance—continue to support legalized abortion until and unless from the pulpit they rage, rage against this blood-soaked execration. In continuing to "clarify" the issues for Catholic voters with carefully measured words, Church leaders will inexorably lead them to vote for the self-righteous left-wingers who demand justice for the marginalized but not for those in the womb. Can I get an amen?

The Devil Went Down to Dixie

Maryland and Louisiana have something in common: Baltimore and New Orleans were both occupied by the Yankees early in the War of Secession. And the Maryland state song was written in Louisiana. But the Pelican State and the Old Line State share more than history; they are bound to each other by religion and ancestry as well. Today visitors to ancient graveyards in Maryland will often find French names carved into tombstones because, Catholic and Southern, Marylanders and Louisianans tended to marry each other. Unfortunately, the same people who presume Maryland to be Northern, also presume that all Southerners are Protestant. But Catholicism though not a dominant faith in the South has not been without some influence here. As the Church in America degenerates, however, it is increasingly at odds with the culture and traditions of the "Christ-haunted" Texas plains and Carolina Low Country; Mississippi Delta and Old Kentucky and Maryland.

Southern Catholics are very different from the Northerners who, having moved to the South, are joining our parishes in great numbers, the Liturgy of the Word often spoiled now by the assertive voice of the Yankee reader. The carpetbaggers in my ancestral parish I can say with some assurance would be more than happy to ignore the fact that their church is a memorial chapel named for Confederate general Frank Crawford Armstrong, who served under Nathan Bedford Forrest. And I can't imagine any of the Catholic newcomers to our county ever tolerating tobacco worms falling on their heads during Mass. This actually happened one year when there was a bumper crop and a lack of barn space in which to house it, one parish priest allowing farmers to hang their tobacco in the rafters of his church.

My rural community has been blessed over the years with priests of this caliber, priests who have loved us, who have loved our Southern agrarian culture, and we have welcomed many holy and brilliant clerics, the most brilliant among them walking with a painful stoop thanks to the "hospitality" of his Japanese captors in the Philippines. Once at Mass, without missing a beat, this father translated into English the New Testament from Greek which version an altar boy by mistake brought to him. But we have had our share of troubled and cruel "missionaries." At a funeral service in the early 1990s, the officiant announced to the mourners that the deceased, an eighteen-year-old boy killed in an automobile accident, was in Hell because he had missed Mass the previous Sunday. The Archdiocese of Washington D.C., made up of the parishes of the District of Columbia and five counties of Maryland's Western Shore, responding to complaints from parishioners, merely transferred this insensitive "eulogist" to another church in Southern Maryland, an unimportant backwater in the eyes of the chancellery.

As with our priests, the nuns who came to our county over the years were mostly good people. At Father Andrew White School in Leonardtown, Maryland, we were taught by the Sisters of Charity of Nazareth, Kentucky, an order founded by Marylander Mother Catherine Spalding. There was only one truly mean soul among them: Sister Mary Imelda. Out on the playground she would throw a "dodge" ball at us hard enough to bruise us, and she once shook my cousin Delores until her nose began to bleed. I was fortunate not to have been her pupil. During the four years I attended FAW,

Maryland, My Maryland

I received a respectable education from lay teachers and Sisters Margaret Regina and Agnes Charles. Their rosary-girded black habits alone putting the fear of God into all of us, they in no manner resembled the feminist religious of today. Our studies, accordingly, were rooted in orthodoxy and in the ancient precepts and magisterium of the Church. While the abuse such as my cousin endured should not be tolerated, and it still saddens me, today too much else is tolerated, and Catholic education now provides little in the way of moral guidance or education for that matter.

Directions for completing a book report form sent home with a Maryland grade schooler instruct: "Please have your child fill in the information regarding their name, the name of the book, and the author by them self. PRACTICE MAKES PERFECT!" Another letter states that on Grandparents Day, visitors may attend Mass with their grandchildren after participating in classroom activities or may meet their "grandchildren at church and then return to school with he/she" for lunch. All writers make careless errors, including the author of this essay who is guilty of splitting infinitives on occasion, but the mistakes in the examples above cannot be blamed on inattentiveness; they more likely arise from a need for remedial grammar lessons and a lack of insight into how phony and absurd feminist inclusionary English sounds. Too often it seems the certification of teachers is divorced from a rigorous academic substrate.

English is not the only problem at parochial schools where politically correct "history" is taught and text books and workbooks promote left-wing causes and multiculturalism. Though the Washington D.C. Archdiocese does a better job educationally than area public schools, a rabid liberalism espoused by primarily Yankee teaching staff and administrators undermines the curricular and the extracurricular as well.

It takes the patience of Job to sit through awards ceremonies that recognize every child in the school, therefore recognizing no one. And there is blatant indoctrination of pupils by some of the bolder leftist Catholic "educators." At one area parochial school, in the fall of 2008, the faculty staged a mock election in which each student was required to declare openly for the Democrat or the Republican candidate. In the highly charged atmosphere, a child supporting McCain was called a racist by a classmate; another felt pressured she said to "vote" for Obama. Overseeing all of this was a principal who proudly displayed a "Hope and Change" bumper sticker on her car. A fan of neither candidate, I believe that this "civics lesson" was inappropriate because there was no secret ballot, and some of the "voters" were held up to ridicule by their peers. But more inappropriate was the school principal's support of a man who believes a child who survives a late-term abortion should be denied medical attention and should be left to die somewhere in a dirty, dark room. Obama's politics cannot be reconciled with the Catholic faith.

When Benedict rose to the papal throne, I was optimistic about the American Church's becoming more conservative, but the hierarchy remained mired in a banal and dangerous secularism. And now there is Francis. God help us. What the Church needs is a physically unbroken, fire-eating pontiff with the voice of a Baptist preacher and the intellect and certitude of a Ratzinger because Catholics seem to be putting up a paltry defense against the "wickedness and snares of the Devil." The faithful in the South, including that bourbon-drinking, tobacco-growing Catholic South I knew as a child, have traditionally been more mindful—and unashamed to admit—that Satan is alive and dwelling among us "seeking the ruin of souls." Flannery O'Connor knew him well: "My Devil has a name, a history and a definite plan. His name is Lucifer, he's a fallen angel, his sin is pride, and his aim is the destruction of the Divine plan."[1] The twenty-first century "enlightened" will scorn the quaint Christianity of O'Connor and her hick "metaphor" Satan at their own peril.

I'm OK, You're…a Yankee

One Easter Sunday I discovered that I had an accent. At my grandmother's house, the children were out on the lawn when a cousin, who had lived abroad, started teasing me about my pronunciation of the word *boiled*—we had been discussing the process of dying the eggs we were collecting in our Easter baskets. She thought I was saying something like *bald*. This incident took place in the late 1950s when people in my rural county were still speaking in the traditional way. But the forces that have now nearly destroyed our Southern language had already been set in motion when, shortly after the attack on Pearl Harbor, the deep waters of the Patuxent River brought the U.S. Navy to us. Before the necessities of the world war disturbed the county's isolation, there were fifteen thousand of us: descendants of English Catholics from Yorkshire and Southern England and of a small scattering of Frenchmen and Scots, descendants of those native people and colonists who married each other from the earliest days of the settlement and of those brought here in chains from Africa. Since then a tidal wave of job seekers has swamped our peninsula increasing the population to around 100,000, and the speech and customs of these newcomers prevail.

In high school in the 1960s, I took my cues from transplanted Yankee students and aligned myself with them against my "backward" fellow Countians, who were, they thought and I thought, "uncultured" and slow-witted. Careful not to slip into my "hayseed" manner of speech and not to invite the carpetbagger "in crowd" home to the tobacco farm where I lived, I managed to fool some of the new ones into accepting me although deep down in my heart I was convinced that I was not their equal.

It was in the supply department at the Patuxent River Naval Air Station, where I had taken a civil service position, that I grew even more ashamed of my plain old country self and my birthplace. While there I learned that people only counted if they came from superior places such as Akron or Cleveland or Allentown, PA. I will never forget the day a co-worker, a New Yorker, "corrected" my accent haughtily informing me that my Southern pronunciation of *pecan* was wrong. The word was *pickahn*, emphasis on the second syllable, not *peacan*,[1] emphasis on the first, she instructed. Turning red, I just stared at her speechless, feeling idiotic.

At least the New Yorkers and the Ohioans coming to the county in those days were paying us the compliment of thinking we were Southern, and, by definition according to them, inferior, but Southern nonetheless. What offended me more than the name calling of the Northerners was the name calling of the transplants from the deeper South. Thinking that the only kind of Southern was Carolinian, Appalachian or Mississippian, they told us, in a jocose way, that we were Yankees. But I didn't find this funny. When I was on the receiving end of this slur, I remained as mute and insulted as I had been when the New Yorker had given me my diction lesson within the dreary confines of the cubicles at stock control.

Though my Beatles-loving baby boomer cohorts and subsequent generations were to be infected greatly by the culture of the Navy base people, those who were born in the 1930s in the county have largely escaped deracination. When they were coming of age, the job-taking intruders were fewer in number and had not had time enough to ruin completely their Southern agrarian community. Even as young adults, those Countians born pre-World War II, when they felt compelled to leave, moved to Washington and Baltimore, cities that in that decade of hula hoops and sock hops were still relatively Southern. But by the late 1960s, all over our region strangers had been telling us for quite some time how we should speak and who we should be.

Our struggles with our identity—and we were struggling whether we knew it or not—cannot be reduced to the oversimplification that we were just bumpkins whose clod-hopper world had been disturbed. Those who invaded our county were also from places like Cresco, Iowa and Turtle Lake, Minnesota. What we were losing was not so much our rurality as our Southernness.

Nowadays the new people—who hate our county but won't leave and won't stop moving here—still laugh at us for being country and for being stupid, but no one bothers much to correct our Southern accent anymore because only a handful of us still have one. At the age of thirty-two, after having lived in the Midwest for over a decade, I came home. Another few years of foundering passed before my eyes were fully opened, and, at long last, I stood up to the cultural cleansers in my state and began the awkward reacquisition of my good manners and language. Today, I allow no one, Southerner or Yankee, to define me or to tell me how to act or how to say *pecan*.

Maryland, My Maryland

Saving Maryland's Southern Speech

One morning, shortly after moving to Little Falls, Minnesota, I was served a fried hot dog and eggs in a small café. What I had asked for, however, was not a hot dog but sausage, which to the Southerner is ground pork in bulk or links highly seasoned with red pepper and sage; to the Midwesterner, including that long-ago waitress who had taken my breakfast order, it is anything in a casing. Ironically, it was my subsequent years on the plains of the Midwest that taught me to appreciate the South and its language.

But it is not fashionable today to be Southern compliments of all those who insist that we are slope-headed morons. Unenlightened and TV-mesmerized, most Americans believe that Northern speech is the norm, and, pressured to speak "properly," each new generation in the South is sounding less Southern, a fact that should warm the Yankee heart. The cultural cleansing that is now starting to affect other Southern states has plagued Maryland for over half a century. A friend of mine, originally from Kentucky, told me that when she learned that her husband's Missouri-based company had transferred him to the Old Line State, she thought she was moving to New England and pictured rocky coastlines and yellow-slickered Captain Quints hauling in their lobster pots. Today she knows better and is a champion of Maryland's embattled Southern culture.

For quite some time now, the very uttering of authentic Maryland speech in, of all places, Maryland has proven comment worthy. *Washington Times* correspondent Jon Ward, in a 2002 article, writes that farmers at a tobacco auction in Upper Marlboro "communicated by mutters and grunts. When they spoke loudly enough to be heard, it was with a distinct Southern twang."[1] That so-called twang was a real Maryland accent. In 1770 William Eddis, an Englishman, was impressed by the loveliness of this now-vanishing native tongue.

Joyce Bennett

In Maryland and throughout the adjacent provinces...it is worthy of observation that a striking similarity of speech universally prevails; and it is strictly true that the pronunciation of the generality of the people has an accuracy and elegance that cannot fail of gratifying the most judicious ear.[2]

Jon Ward's "Southern-sounding" farmers today strangers in their own land, their speech has been replaced by the annoying parlance of the Harry Reids and the Rudy Giulianis and, more and more, by the nondescript "accents" of those who could be from almost anywhere. Marylanders who speak in the old way, the ones who say *over yonder*, who stress the first syllable, who call *dinner supper*, are a curiosity now and often the targets of insults and attempts at "re-education."

The desire to destroy the speech of perceived inferiors is nothing new. Centuries ago the Romanized English waged war on the language of the Welsh and the Cornish, the Highland Scots and the Irish. The League of the South, founded in 1994 to preserve the culture and sovereignty of the American Southland, has patterned its own hedge schools after those established by the Irish to protect their identity and to fight the cultural cleansing imposed on them by the English. The term hedge school originates in the secretive teaching of Ireland's language, as well as religion and history, to children literally in the shadow of a hedge row.

"Elocutionists" Thomas Sheridan and John Walker were among the self-appointed language reformers of the 1700s. They were, according to James Brieg, "adept at helping immigrants scrub away their Irish and Scottish accents. Burrs seemed to be particularly offensive."[3] There are still 'Enry 'Igginses in England deciding what is and isn't an "acceptable" accent. But it would be a terrible loss to true linguistic diversity if the Eastenders of London, among others, ever started "talkin' right."

Fortunately, ancient language forms survive in spite of linguistic chauvinism. McCrum and fellow researchers, whose book on the subject of English advances the false notion that the "Southern accent" is almost exclusively African in origin,[4] were surprised to discover in the 1970s "strangely enough...here and there...some tantalizing, fragmentary evidence of the lost voices of the early Americans."⁵ But concerning the phonological anachronisms found on Tangier Island in the Chesapeake Bay, they were I believe overly optimistic.

> *Tangier is part of the state of Virginia, but its English shares many characteristics with the most isolated communities of the Atlantic seaboard. Together with the other Piedmont/Tidewater districts, and the "hoi toiders" or "bankers" of Okrakoke/ Roanoke, North Carolina, it forms one of the most vivid parts of the fossilized English language on the eastern seaboard of the United States. The variety of English spoken on Tangier is not threatened with extinction. The speech of the young people is as strong and distinctive as their grandparents'. It will surely last into the twenty-first century.⁶*

It is true that the English of the Tangerines, which is similar in many ways to that of certain areas of Maryland, has lasted into the twenty-first century, but just barely, their young no less susceptible to the forces of deracination than their mainland peers. The last time I went to Tangier, about ten years ago, I was told by one of those golf cart guides who give tours of the island that the local dialect was changing "thanks" to television.

Even in the face of such detrimental influences, the language of the colonists of Virginia and Maryland is taking a very long time to die out in what are considered the more remote areas of the two states. One gentleman to whom I was introduced a few years ago at a government-funded "assisted living facility" was doing his part to keep it alive. Shuffling down a gloomy, plywood-paneled hallway with the aid of an aluminum walker, he spoke with an unspoiled Maryland accent so pretty I couldn't keep my mind on what he was saying because I was listening so intently to how he was saying it.

Evidence of Maryland's connections to Virginia is to be found everywhere. Al Gough, the estimable, long-time editor of *Chronicles of St. Mary's*, told me that when he was in the military in the 1960s and stationed at Ft. Jackson, South Carolina, his instructor, who was from the Tar Heel State, on first hearing him speak, commented that he must have come from the Northern Neck of Virginia or from St. Mary's County, Maryland because of the way Al pronounced the word *house*. His lieutenant joked, "It's been a while since a young lady invited me to her 'hoase.'" Just to hear the sound again, he asked Al to say, "The mouse ran about the house." Yet another friend of mine, a Marylander, visiting High Point, North Carolina with her husband, met and had a conversation with a well-spoken, well-educated lady, a native North Carolinian, who, noticing my friend's way of pronouncing *out oat* remarked that she had the most beautiful "Virginia accent." It is an accent not heard much lately. On election night 2009, Fox News Channel's Frank Luntz watched election returns with a group of "Virginians" in the Richmond area. His remark that he was "in the South not the Washington suburbs" was noteworthy because out of the entire focus group gathered that evening to give Luntz feedback only one person spoke with a Southern let alone a Virginia accent. Richmond is as much Yankee-occupied as are the D.C. suburbs.

It was on one of my frequent visits to Robert E. Lee's birthplace that I reconfirmed the similarity in the way people from Virginia's Northern Neck and my own St. Mary's County speak. Touring Stratford Hall that day, I fell in with a group of people from New Jersey. Of African descent, the native Virginian interpreting the kitchen area was explaining to us the operation of the spit in the big kitchen hearth. In early days, game birds and chickens would be skewered and roasted slowly over the fire, a little dog pulling a rope back and forth to activate a device that turned the spit. When the uncomprehending Yankee tourists kept asking our docent to repeat the word *dog* over and over, I volunteered as interpreter. The docent was saying *dug*, the same pronunciation I grew up hearing across the river in Maryland.

Isolated for so long from the rest of the world, St. Mary's County is not only a good place to find Maryland's colonial language forms but to find as well the regionalisms thought of as exclusive to the Deep South. The older members of my extended family, some of whom are embarrassed by their Southern—or, to their way of thinking, country—roots have nonetheless helped me to discover more about those very roots. In her late eighties, my great-aunt Aggie, after fifty years in Washington State, came home. She and I had in common our former expatriation from the South. I learned from her that when she was newly arrived in the Northwest in the 1940s, people poked fun at her for her courtesy and her accent calling her *honey chile*. While that was a compliment, she took it as a criticism and eventually "adapted" and grew "less Southern." Sadly, I was guilty of the same thing. The difference is that unlike her great-niece she never understood what she had allowed to happen to herself. She wasn't angry at it as I was.

My mother, though indifferent to my campaign to keep Maryland Southern, has been nevertheless a tremendous help to me. She was the one who told me that St. Mary's Countians used *rinch* for *rinse*, and she confirmed also something that my Aunt Elizabeth had said about the old expression, *I'm fixin|* (to do this or that). My aunt, who passed away in her late nineties not that long ago, informed me that people in St. Mary's used *I'm fixin|* routinely. Fluent in Spanish and widely traveled—she spent many years in Europe and South America—she retained much of her Southern manner of speech, and in particular the South still could be heard in her pronunciation of the short *i* as *ee*. My maternal grandmother, Madeleine Thompson Cusic, also pronounced *fish* as *feesh*, *dish* as *deesh*. And I have heard others say *eech* for *itch* and *artifeeshal* for *artificial*.

I have run across many Maryland regionalisms in the works of Southern writers. In her correspondence,[7] Flannery O'Connor speaks of being "broke out with" phonograph records, meaning that she had an abundance of them. In Maryland there are still people who would say of a lottery winner that he or she is broke out with money. The "hillbilly Thomist" also in her letters uses, in a light-hearted vein, the Maryland-Georgia colloquialisms "Sareday" for *Saturday* and "tomatuses" for *tomatoes*.

Chaps, a word meaning young children, has not entirely disappeared in Southern Maryland. And it shows up in William Faulkner's "Spotted Horses."

Flem had one of these little striped sacks of Jody Varner's candy... He put the sack into Mrs. Armstid's hand, like he would have put it into a hollow stump...' A little sweetening for the chaps,' he says.[8]

Clearly linking Maryland's speech to Britain's, *chaps* will always be to me an endearing way to address little ones, far better than the Yankee's *kids*, which Flannery O'Connor considered "low-class" and "urban." My grandmother Madeleine didn't like the word either. According to my mother, she once became very angry because an intoxicated man of lower social rank had the nerve to instruct her to tell her "kids" to run an errand for him. His presumption had not offended her as much as his referring to her children in such a familiar and ill-bred manner.

Chaps isn't found in Margaret Mitchell's *Gone With the Wind*, but there are in the novel many other Marylandisms as well as general allusions to the Old Line State.[9] Mitchell describes retreating Confederate troops as "bearded, shabby files," marching down Atlanta's Peachtree Street "to the tune of 'Maryland! My Maryland!'" Because she was writing in the 1930s, Mitchell was not that far removed from the war and was able to put into the mouths of her characters the dialect of those who had actually lived it. Her characters are fictional, but not their speech.

Mammy's "Bress Gawd" reminds me of the way older Marylanders, particularly black Marylanders, say *Bless God*. Allowing Scarlett to comment on the linguistic diversity of the South, Mitchell inadvertently draws a connection between the speech of South Carolina and that of lower Tidewater Maryland. Scarlett, greatly preferring new Atlanta to old Charleston and accustomed to the "brisk voices of upland Georgia," cannot tolerate the "drawling flat voices of the low country" of Carolina which speech Scarlet considers an "affectation." She ridicules their saying "paam" for *palm*. Among watermen in Maryland, I am told, there were until the early 1960s those who said *cam as the pam of your hand*, and Outer Bankers in North Carolina to this day use *slickcam* for *slick calm*. Outsider Scarlet also mocks the Low Country's pronunciation of *house* as "hoose," calling to mind that linguistic idiosyncrasy of Northern Neck Virginians and St. Mary's Countians I mentioned above.

As a Marylander I know what Margaret Mitchell's characters are doing when I read that they "pulled faces" or they "made pallets" on the floor in anticipation of house guests. Prissy's "amberlance," Scarlet's "Name of God" and many pronunciations, words and expressions found in *GWTW* are still in use in rural Maryland today.

But ignorance is hard at work wiping out the old speech. Dr. Seth Lerer makes the point that a Southernism is "not a question of illiteracy; it is not a question of inability; it's a question of a kind of fossil moment in the history of pronunciation."[10] My mother has been ridiculed for her use of older forms, was ridiculed by a carpetbagger woman for pronouncing the word *humble* as *'umble*. That woman had assumed that the silent *h* was proof of an unschooled mind—something that would come as a surprise to the Frenchman. As for me, I can't bring myself to say *a historic*.

On two occasions, I have heard Northern newcomers, who pride themselves in their "tolerance," reveal a deep-seated racism when they deride locals in my county for sounding "like black people." Of course, there is a reason for this: Many of us are black people. More importantly, Southern natives—black and white—share a common linguistic tradition. I believe that the old language is more purely preserved in the speech of African-Americans, and those who love that language are in their debt. Those white Southerners who remain true to their culture will share phonological characteristics with black Southerners who are speaking the same Southern English ultimately rooted in Anglo-Celtic languages.

I have always been struck by the fact that the globe-trotting Northerner who gushes over a Scottish or Devonshire accent will condemn the same accent in the mouth of a Southerner. Cantankerous, tin-eared Yankees believe that Northern speech is refined; Southern ain't. This is a false dichotomy. A Northerner can fracture the language, but because he has "that way of speaking" the assumption is that he is more learned than the well-read Southerner. Barack Obama is considered an elegant and educated speaker, but he frequently makes subject-verb agreement and other errors which are overlooked in part because they are spoken with his rather irritating Yankee accent. A more eloquent or dignified speaker than an unreconstructed upper-class Southerner, however, is rare. Yankees think Southern people are backward because they don't understand our idiom, meiosis, litotes, hyperbole or enallage. Only a Southerner will truly understand that *there ain't nothing wrong with the radio* means *the radio represents a technological feat of extraordinary proportions.*

While this highly evolved and richly textured Southern language has been in peril for some time, all across America organic regional dialects are threatened with extinction. Because for many years I have cared for an elderly family member who is a fan of only one channel, I have had the chance to listen to or watch hundreds of hours of the tackiest of TV programming. While at times it has required extreme patience to look at one more installment of *Match Game 76*, to hear one more salacious innuendo from snickering celebrity has-beens, my reluctant viewing of or listening to the Game Show Network's offerings (reruns and new shows) has enabled me to conduct, almost in self-defense, a sort of sociological study. I realized that over the last several decades not only have these programs served as leftist propaganda vehicles, they have chronicled the very cultural decline they have helped to bring about.

That America grows coarser and dumber by the day is obvious, but what I have noticed as well is that the game show contestants of the 1970s were more likely to have distinct regional accents. Back then, the Bronx was the Bronx; Savannah was Savannah. And the *Match Game* stars could always be counted on to make fun of the drawl of a Texan or Tennessean who was willing to play the fool for a few Yankee dollars, unashamed to debase himself if that is what it took to win. *Family Feud* host Richard Dawson, a rabid left winger and an unpleasant man, when he wasn't proselytizing on behalf of liberal causes, routinely scoffed at Southern speech and was at times openly hostile to the Southerners who appeared on his show. He wouldn't have much to scoff at today because in more recent times most game show contestants, even those who say they are from the South, sound Northern.

Maryland, My Maryland

The Southern language is not dead, however, and could flourish again if we would have the courage to speak it. Ten years in the Upper Midwest deprived me of my own accent, but since I returned to Maryland, I have mainly associated with unreconstructed natives (who, some say, sound "half Southern, half Australian"), and it is gradually coming back to me judging from the fact that Yankees are more condescending towards me and are remarking more often about my speech. It turns out that I didn't even have to move so far from home to learn a new way of talking. Most of my siblings (I have seven) now imitate the carpetbaggers in our county. One of my brothers even became testy when I asked him why he has replaced *y'all* with *you guys*. Some in my family think that I should not speak "country" because I "know better."

I have had to resort to a deliberate effort to develop again the habit of employing that Southern contraction I used so naturally from an early age. My grandchildren say it most of the time in spite of the disapproval of some of their classmates and Northern teachers, who tell them that only ignorant people say *y'all* or that it should be said "only at home."

I recall one of those anti-*y'all* Yankee school teachers, who apparently can't find work north of the Mason-Dixon, mocking a local man whose account of a severe storm had been quoted in a county newspaper. The Yankee, who was attending the same party as I, had read the article and deemed hilarious the yokel's declaration that the tornado was "just a twistin'" as it skimmed the treetops before blowing over the Patuxent River and into the next county.

The storm spotter the Yankee party goer found so amusing could have taken several words to describe the event, but his reaction was economically expressed by "archaic" verb augmentation. He was commenting both on the incredible nature of the storm and his amazement at it. It was a twistin'! The need for clarity of expression is the reason Southerners favor such language devices and why they use *y'all* rather than *you* to indicate more than one person. A language that can communicate ever finer distinctions is a superior language and should be preserved, should be spoken even if Yankees laugh, especially if Yankees laugh.

Joyce Bennett

Old Versus New Baltimore

In 1812 Light Horse Harry Lee narrowly escaped death at the hands of a prowar mob in the same city that would remember his son in the late 1940s with one of the South's most magnificent Confederate monuments. But through the ensuing decades, in spite of sometimes-rowdy slum dwellers, Baltimore calmed down and became a more civilized place. Like New Orleans, however, its culture and language were destined to be corrupted by the influence of the Stanley Kowalskis, the Apeneck Sweeneys, who were to inundate "Crab Town."

Baltimore, whose financial district was once known as the Wall Street of the South, has been home to Southern luminaries such as Edgar Allan Poe, Basil Gildersleeve and Confederate Major Richard Venable, who was one of the city's—and the South's—most distinguished attorneys. The auburn-haired Hetty Cary, the "handsomest woman in the Southland" according to Henry Kyd Douglas,[1] called it home as well.

During the War of Secession, Fannie A. Beers, a Northerner married to a Confederate soldier, passed through the town and observed the reaction of Baltimoreans to Federal invasion.

> *Arrived in Baltimore, we found ourselves among those whose hearts were filled with ardent love of "the Cause," and bitter hatred for the soldiers who had, in spite of their heroic resistance, so lately passed through the streets of the city on their way to subjugate the South.*[2]

It was this Baltimore that turned out to wave a bon voyage to Confederate spy Rose Greenhow as she stood on the deck of the Yankee vessel that was to deliver her to "exile" in Virginia. It was this Baltimore that so enraged Beast Butler he threatened to raze it with cannon fire.

A growing German population had begun changing the city even before the Yankees invaded it, but in the early-twentieth century many more immigrants arrived to fill heavy industrial jobs. They were the ancestors of the Barbara Mikulskis and the Nancy Pelosis. By the 1960s what was left of Baltimore's Southern culture was embodied in an aging minority of Baltimoreans which included the Blounts, a brother and sister who lived in one of the city's iconic brick row houses. Speaking in the soft English of the Upper South, Mr. Blount always wore an immaculate necktie, vest and coat, and, no matter how warm the weather, he would never be caught in his shirt sleeves receiving visitors. Blount and his sister, Emily, in a hat she would not remove until she was in the privacy of her own home, dined at Love's and Miller Brothers, restaurants that dated back to the steamboat days.

By the 1990s the Baltimore of the Blounts was a fading memory. In an article in *Baltimore Magazine*, a young Mississippi woman studying medicine at The Hopkins and moonlighting at a kitschy restaurant called Savannah is credited with introducing Baltimoreans to the "Southern experience," to being "nice."[3] Shrill, pushy carpetbaggers, especially the women, would, admittedly, be in need of such a lesson. But Marylanders like Hetty Cary and Emily Blount would not have required tutoring from Mississippians regarding manners and charm.

Southernness was a way of life in Old Baltimore; it is a marketing gimmick in New Baltimore. H.L. Mencken, a second-generation German born in the 1880s, was a witness to and commentator on the "evolution" of the town. Mencken spent much of his time eating and drinking at Baltimore's Hotel Rennert which billed itself as The Standard Hotel of the South. He might have been aware of this, but he seemed to think of most of Maryland as Northern and the Eastern Shore as somehow aberrantly Southern. What Mencken has to say about Maryland's linguistic forms in *The American Language* does not ring quite true. Until recently the speech of the bulk of the people "around the periphery of Washington" was not "North Midland, with a few touches of Southern,"[4] as Mencken writes, but purely Southern. My uncle Robert Hicks, born in the 1920s in the D.C. area, did not pronounce *caught cot* and had a Southern accent that rivaled any Virginian's. And even Maryland's suburban and Yankeefied Montgomery County, the majority of its population Northerners (and a growing number of illegal immigrants), is still home to a handful of beleaguered throwback Southerns.

Inaccurate also is Mencken's assertion that the contraction *y'all* is used "south" of the Potomac while the form *yous* predominates "north" of it (Ibid., 548). But when I was growing up in Maryland or, as Mencken would have it, "super-Potomac," I would have thought anyone saying *yous* was from another planet. While it is true that it is heard in some New Baltimore enclaves, it has hardly been the standard in the city for the second-person plural. The speech of certain Baltimoreans, for example, Dundalkians, has always sounded strange to most other Marylanders.

Characterizing the use of the terms *yonder* and *to carry* in the sense of *to convey* as typical of the deeper South (Ibid.,450), Mencken must never have visited my home county. In describing what is Southern, he uses many Maryland regionalisms: the dropping of the final *r*, an old Maryland apocope; the elimination of the *r* sound after *th* as in *thow* for *throw*; the "*y* glide before *u* after *t, n* and *d*" as in *tyune* for *tune* (Ibid., 462). These are all now nearly extinct Marylandisms.

Though he admired the antebellum aristocracy of the Southland, Mencken seems to have had no affection for the postbellum South. And he definitely preferred a Yankee Maryland to one that was Southern—it was, after all, his latecomer ilk who have striven to Northernize our state. Further, because Baltimore's German community was careful to preserve its own native culture, Mencken himself spoke "Northern." His was the accent of the Michigander.[5] Possessed of the cultural cleanser's animus towards the defiantly unreconstructed Eastern Shore, he considered it a land of "morons" and "malarious peasants." Today's New Baltimoreans also despise the Shoremen, but they love the "peasantry's" scenic waterfront, which they, along with New Yorkers and Philadelphians, are buying up at an alarming rate. The displacement of the Maryland people continues.

Maryland, My Maryland

Halfbacks and Wannabes

My mother had to have some physical therapy a few years ago, and this is how we came to know Debbie, a physical therapy assistant. Two times a week she would visit and work with Mama to get her back on her feet. Chatty and friendly and certainly dedicated to her important calling, she had an irritating propensity, however, to characterize my mother and me as Northerners and herself as Southern. But we never determined whence Debbie had sprung: We thought at first Illinois, then she mentioned Kentucky. I believe she was a Kentuckian on some days but not on others. What I heard in her voice, I think, was Southern Illinois. Debbie is not exceptional: The Old Line State seems to have its share of wannabe-Southerner carpetbaggers these days.

Content to be Yankees, the Northerners who have never lived in the South before moving to rural Maryland are happy just to lord their superiority over us, artlessly broadcasting to the other diners at the local French restaurant that *les huitres* were better in Paris last year. They think that we denizens of God's Little Acre are impressed with them and their travels abroad.

I know better how to deal with this variety of Northerner than I do halfbacks, the Yankees who relocate to places like Florida and South Carolina for a year or two and then move to one of the border states, usually Maryland. While living farther south, they learn from the natives that being a Yankee isn't a good thing, which is true, and that Maryland is somewhere near Rhode Island, which is false. When these relocating Yankees move to the Old Line State, they hatch the plan to pass themselves off as Southern. In the frigid voices of New England or the whine of the Upper Midwest, though they were raised in little frozen burgs in charmless houses with three-foot icicles perpetually hanging off the eaves, they love to complain about the cold weather "up here" in

Maryland whose weather is no colder than that of the rest of the Upper South.

I once had a run in with the transplanted editor of a local newspaper who, referring to Maryland as the "near north," condescendingly explained to his readers what soul food is and that in the South people eat something called greens. He also "enlightened" us on the Southern pronunciation of *chitterlings*. At the time I was writing an intermittent column for a rival newspaper and took the opportunity to respond in an open letter to this self-described Southerner (he said he had been raised in Nashville).

> *Ethnic Marylanders...have always enjoyed greens and fatback, cornbread, ribs, chitlins (we know how the word is pronounced) and pigs feet and more.... If you read old...cookbooks, you will find that Maryland cuisine is included in the "Food of the South" sections....Our Maryland beaten biscuits and fried chicken were especially treasured...years ago....And... African Americans did not bring "soul food" up here from the "Deep South"; We aren't Detroit...as a matter of fact, we exported our culinary traditions to other Southern states....And Ethnic Marylanders who also happen to be black people have been here since the 17th century.*

A few years later, by chance, I had an opportunity to hear this "Tennessean" speak, and his voice was unmistakably Northern.

The most bizarre illustration of Yankee pretense I have ever observed, however, involved my brother Charles, a Viet Nam vet and charter boat captain among other things. Charles is not interested in or even aware of his Southern heritage and is very much taken with carpetbagger culture. But he still speaks with a Southern accent, though it is tainted with Northernisms. One day I happened to be present when my brother had struck up a conversation with a young woman who, in replying to his question, said that she was from Georgia. Charles then remarked, "Oh you are from the South." In turn this woman, in the blandest Northern-speak, responded to my Southern-talking brother, "Yes, I'm a Southern girl." In other words, the Southerner was pretending to be the Yankee; the Yankee was pretending to be the Southerner. It is truly an upside-down world, a world in which Newt Gingrich is Southern, Steny Hoyer is Northern (while I despise their politics equally, at least Steny is not a Yankee; Gingrich is).

But the worst of the impostors try to affect a Southern accent and unasked instruct us how to say *Louisville* and *New Orleans* (Yankees are trying too hard when they say *Nawlins*—only bona fide Louisianans know how it is really pronounced). I suppose it is a compliment to the South that they wish to be Southern, but they won't fool most of us natives. One day Debbie, our PT assistant, thought she would expound on the subject of the South, in particular the Southerner's use of the expression *bless his heart* sometimes to soften a criticism. She proceeded to quote from some comedian who had built a routine around the saying. The rules of Southern courtesy prevented me from showing my irritation—and I was irritated—so I just smiled and hoped that she would leave soon. I did manage a weak "We say that too," but she didn't hear me.

Debbie is not in the strict sense a halfback, but she is a wannabe. Her presumptions about Marylanders are hard to take because she isn't Southern and we aren't Yankees, and we don't appreciate our being maligned that way. My Confederate great-great-grandfathers are turning in their graves.

As most people, Debbie is unread and therefore would not have known our history or our location on a map, but she could have noticed that Mama and I say *y'all* and that she says *you guys*. She could have noticed that we eat biscuits and grits (sometimes she arrived at meal time). She could have noticed the pictures of Generals Lee and Jackson and the Confederate cuckoo clock on the wall. But she didn't. She was too busy acting out her lines to reflect on where she was or to whom she was speaking. But on further reflection and in the spirit of Christian charity, I guess there are worse fates than having to play the Yankee to Miss Debbie's Southern belle—bless her heart.

Joyce Bennett

Name of God...Yankee Ham Hocks!

One Sunday I decided to make collard greens. Southerners love an old-time boiled dinner (or supper) with cornbread or biscuits and cucumbers in vinegar. Sometimes we season our mess of greens with fatback or a streak-of-lean-streak-of-fat, but I had chosen ham hocks this particular day. In good spirits as I started cooking my collards, I soon realized that something was not right.

In fact, I had just begun simmering the ham hocks for a few minutes to extract the essence of their curing when I realized that rather than the aroma of aged seasoning meat steaming up from the pot bringing back memories of my grandmother Blanche Nash Bennett and her old-fashioned kitchen, there was instead a damp unpleasantness hanging in the air. By degrees, it dawned on me that I had inadvertently purchased Yankee ham hocks! It was too late to make a return trip to the store so there were to be no greens for that Sunday's dinner.

Finding good seasoning meat is more and more difficult these days in Maryland. When I was young, even when we weren't living on the farm, my family kept hogs, raising them humanely and dispatching them to their Maker with swift mercy. They were hogs who were loved, who had their backs scratched and their meal gently stirred with water in their trough. They were not the hogs who were loaded on big trucks to take them to their mass slaughter in some big cold Midwestern town. My father had to hire a neighbor to kill them in the fall because he couldn't do it having developed such an affection for these intelligent animals.

By raising our own pigs, we could just go out to the meat house and get that nice yellowing salty slab of fatback to season our greens. And fatback was a delicacy my grandmother often served instead of store-bought bacon. Sliced up and cooked until crisp, it makes the best grease in which to fry eggs, imparting a wonderful "country" flavor to them. My grandmother's fatback and eggs, biscuits with molasses and her sweet, strong Puerto Rican coffee are to me Old Maryland. After the interminable, humid summer nights I spent with her, I welcomed the warm fresh mornings sitting at her table breathing in the fragrance of fatback renderings and her McCormick-spice permeated pantry. From June to August, breakfast is the best time of day on a tobacco farm in the Upper South.

The proper preparation of food has not been an inconsequential matter to Southerners, and Yankees might be surprised to learn that many Southern men, even the gun-toting, four-wheel driving tough boys, excel in the culinary arts. But Yankee women old and young think it is cute to announce that they don't cook. A reformed and repentant feminist myself, I never repudiated cooking even at my most radical. I am honored that there are members of my own family who are reluctant to eat any chicken or potato salad other than mine. And in fact the prospect of eating the nasty chunky Northern version of the former or the hard little cubes of potato swimming in a sweetish yellow soup that pass for the latter in the North makes Southern people queasy.

But, as Maryland grows more Yankeefied, fewer grocers carry the basic ingredients— white cornmeal, lard, self-rising flour—that Southern cooks require. Because it stocks my kind of makings, I often buy my groceries at Food Lion. In my home county, there are some small, independently owned grocery stores that still purchase hams and other cuts of meat from a Richmond wholesaler who honors Southern tradition. I have learned, however, to shop more carefully in the Northern-based super stores. Unless on its label a package of seasoning meat bears a trusted Southern brand name, I won't touch it because, as God is my witness, I will never buy Yankee ham hocks again.

The Southerner's Love Affair with the Tomato

On a Baltimore AM station I once heard a radio spot advertising a natural food supplement that provides, apparently, all the benefits of a diet rich in lycopene. The standard American voice in the commercial, in making the case for the convenience of the product, asked (and I am paraphrasing),

"After all, who wants to eat that many tomatoes?" and "Give me a break, tomatoes for breakfast?" But in a more distant Baltimore, a place where fried chicken, biscuits and black-eyed peas were standard fare, in a more distant Maryland, the tomato was as likely to show up at breakfast as at dinner or supper.

Growing up in Southern Maryland, I remember eating tomatoes on many mornings. In the summer and fall, cooks like my mother and my Aunt Delma would slice them up straight off the vine still warm from the sun. For breakfast and for dinner, Mama would often make biscuit and tomato "sandwiches" for us. Using lard as the shortening, she would mix up the biscuit dough out of Richfood self-rising flour and milk, shaping the biscuits by hand and making an indentation in them with her thumb. After she baked the biscuits, she'd split and butter them, putting a slice of ripe tomato in each one.

The best way to prepare green tomatoes is, of course, to fry them, and I frequently fix this dish using my mother's recipe. She did not, however, actually use green but rather very firm tomatoes that had just started turning and showed a hint of yellow and red. Following her recipe, I sprinkle slices of tomato on both sides with salt and sugar, then bread them in a mixture of white cornmeal and flour. I fry them until golden brown in hot grease (preferably lard) and serve them for both dinner and supper.

Cooks in the Upper South long ago devised an ingenious way to use up the bounty of the growing season by making green tomato preserves, another excellent accompaniment to the biscuit, and my paternal grandmother put up many jars of this unexpectedly sweet and delicious compote.

Though recipes for tomato gravy can be found in any Southern cookbook, my mother didn't prepare it that I can recall. But she did serve us stewed tomatoes almost weekly. Not a practitioner of low-fat cooking, she made this by adding to mashed up canned tomatoes about a stick of butter along with bread crumbs, sugar and salt.

Southern cooks can create extraordinary dishes from a few "matuses," some flour or cornmeal and fat because great Southern cooking, just as

French provincial cooking, relies more on skill and passion than a large array of ingredients. The cuisine of the South has been greatly influenced by the poverty suffered in the region during and following the War of Secession. It is fortunate that there is little that is as good as a biscuit-tomato sandwich because sometimes that is all some have had to eat. It is ingrained in the Southern spirit that deprivation is no excuse to abandon graciousness and civilized behavior. This self-disciplined approach to life is why even in the poorest homes in the South the table has been set properly, and the manners have been correct. Southerners are people who rise to the occasion, the same people who danced at starvation balls during the great war and the cruel blockade of the Yankee.

Maryland Cookin'

A woman from Norway told me that when she moved to Maryland in the 1940s, because the Confederate Cross of St. Andrew seemed to be flying everywhere, she mistook it for the state's official flag. The Maryland to which she was introduced is documented in unreconstructed histories, personal memoirs, letters and in old cookbooks. Below (and above) the Mason-Dixon, Maryland was once famous not only for crab dishes but for its fried chicken, beaten biscuits and stuffed ham. And many well-loved Kentucky bourbons are made from old Maryland recipes. People in the Old Line State were sipping on mint juleps long before the first Marylander emigrated to the Dark and Bloody Ground.

Because of my love of cooking, at an office Christmas gift exchange one year, a co-worker thoughtfully gave me a collection of recipes written by a well-known TV personality. But I eventually donated the book to a charity thrift store. It mentions Maryland merely in passing (a sentence or two) and incorrectly states that, as Northerners, Marylanders primarily use salt and black pepper for seasonings. I kept it on the shelf for a while out of respect to my co-worker, but I had an urge to throw it out the window.

Joyce Bennett

Maryland's is not a Northern cuisine. The once-vibrant Southern culture of the state is evident in those quaint "receipt" books that were sold to raise funds for churches and organizations around our state. *A Taste of the Past*, published by the Surratt Society of Charles County, includes dishes such as Confederate Fruit Cake, Jeff Davis Custard Pie and Robert E. Lee Punch.[1]

It was not that long ago that our recipes were routinely incorporated in Southern cookbooks. One I found somewhere along the way is actually a booklet entitled *Southern Style*. Published in 1987 and edited by a North Carolinian, it acknowledges Maryland's superb seafood and features our Chesapeake Crab Imperial.[2]

I was surprised, however, to find Maryland recipes in *Southern Living*'s *The Deep South Cookbook*, published in 1976, though, according to the editors, *Deep South* is not as much a geographical reference as a cultural one.

> *The appreciation of fine foods grown locally was typical of the Maryland people. Later generations would be people who were just as swift to enjoy the land and the fine foods it produced as their ancestors had been. These people would create recipes using those foods, recipes destined to become famous throughout the Deep South and to contribute much to what would one day be a definite Deep South cookery.* [3]

While it is an honor to be included in *SL*'s book, Maryland is an Upper Tidewater not a Deep South state. I do not agree, however, with one Southern writer's contention that *Southern Living* magazine itself erroneously includes Marylanders in its readership in a cynical attempt to increase profit margins. *SL*'s publishers may or may not be avaricious, but they rightly consider the Old Line State Southern. And the *Deep South Cookbook* pays Maryland nothing more than her due.

There are seven recipes credited to the Old Line State in *The Progressive Farmer*'s *Southern Country Cookbook*, published in 1972, the best among them a recipe for the uniquely delicious stuffed ham,[4] which originated (although Charles and Calvert Countians might disagree) in my own St. Mary's County. *Southern Country Cookbook* also features a Mississippi stuffed ham recipe that while not quite like that of my state points to a Southern tradition of ham stuffing,[5] a tradition handed down from British ancestors. There are those who believe that Maryland stuffed ham was a dish created in colonial days by kitchen slaves. Because their household had grown tired of the cured meats that they had eaten all winter, around Easter time, they were said to have gathered spring onions and watercress and, running a knife down into a country ham to make several deep pockets, had stuffed the greens into the meat and boiled it.

When I was coming along, we used slightly different greens for stuffing and placed our ham in a cotton pillow case to keep everything together during the cooking. At first people stuffed "old" hams but because they were too "dear," partially cured or corned hams (which bear no resemblance in flavor to Yankee corned beef) were used in later years. Cured or partially cured with salt, sugar and sometimes red pepper, St. Mary's County country hams are not as a rule smoked. Hams that are to be stuffed must never be smoked, and the fat and rind of them should always be left on as these give the dish its rustic flavor.

Recipes from the Old Line State were not just appreciated by the editors of Southern collections but frequently made their way into publications such as the *Saturday Evening Post*'s *All American Cookbook*. Making room for Maryland Honey Spiced Country Ham along with the Virginia Peanut Soup and the Tennessee Sweet Potato Pudding,[6] *All American Cookbook*, the illustrations in which alone are reason enough to own a copy, seems out of place today considering its "archaic" notions about the geographical boundaries of the Southland and the origins of great Southern cooking. Calling beaten biscuits "the pride of the South," *AAC* offers Maryland's rendition of this most challenging of Southern foods.[7] *AAC* has a special place in my kitchen library because it was written and published by those sufficiently educated to recognize a people who had so greatly influenced Southern—and American—culture.

> *Maryland can boast of one of the most lavish cooking records in the country. In a state literally of milk and honey plus all manner of agricultural and natural abundance, where many large mansions staffed with countless servants in the eighteenth and*

nineteenth centuries made a business of producing extraordinary and historical meals, it is small wonder that so many fine recipes can trace their origin to that fair state.[8]

Maryland's cuisine is now as misunderstood as her history, the former reduced by one "Tennessean" to meat loaf and tuna salad.

As much a history as a cookbook, *Maryland's Way* chronicles life in the land of "pleasant living," of fox hunting and jousting, gentlemen's clubs and grand, antebellum homes. Among the recipes for Muskrat Tred Avon, Poke Salad and Confederate Waffles, are Audrey Bodine's black and white photographs capturing a Southern people and a Southern landscape of low country and rolling hills.

S. B. Buckner's 1937 not-quite-tongue-in-cheek recipe for the "quintessence of gentlemanly beverages" illustrates that which Maryland has tragically forfeited in favor of a new and coarser culture:

> *A mint julep is not the product of a formula. It is a ceremony and must be performed by a gentleman possessing a true sense of the artistic, a deep reverence for the ingredients and a proper appreciation of the occasion. It is a rite that must not be entrusted to a novice, a statistician nor a Yankee. It is a heritage of the old South, an emblem of hospitality and a vehicle in which noble minds can travel together upon the flower-strewn paths of happy and congenial thought....blended by the deft touches of a skilled hand, you have a beverage appropriate for honorable men and beautiful women.*[9]

Yankee feminists will find such old-fashioned "chauvinism" demeaning, but Southern women, beautiful and otherwise, will love this recipe.

Missing from *Maryland's Way*, however, is a recipe for the preparation of possum, the sharp-nosed marsupial with a comical face and close-set eyes that gets into trash cans around the Southern home at night when everyone is asleep. There is nothing cuter than a baby possum and to the hardy few nothing tastier than its mother.

A few autumns ago, some friends of mine attended a storytelling festival at a local church. The people who told the tales were from farther south of Maryland and wondered if way up here in "the North" we had ever seen a possum. When I heard about this incident, I was immediately reminded of an old recipe of my maternal grandmother.

> *First catch a possum and pen him up for a few days feeding him on a diet of bread and water. Then kill and dress him out. Put the possum in a pan and roast him along with some sweet potatoes.*

She also had a way with coconut cake, sweet potato pie and oyster fritters, the Maryland way.

Pickin' Crabs

The Southerner's unhurried approach to life is viewed by Yankees as a sign of cultural inferiority. But in the South, we consider the manic Northerner uncouth and understand that civilized people value restorative repose: We take time to sit on porches to "rest our bones." We live a more contemplative, more intelligent life. While we love NASCAR, we are not speed demons, and, on long road trips, typically stop to look at scenery or have a cup of coffee in a café not in a careening car after a quick stop at the "drive thru." Yankees like to brag about how fast they traveled from some point A to some point B. Snapping their fingers at over-worked waitresses, they demand ever prompter service in restaurants. Even when not on the road, they consider a meal something to get through as quickly as possible. But Southerners linger over supper. We pick pig and visit; we pick crabs and visit.

One day many years ago, after work I went to a crab house in Southern Maryland with a group of education professionals, all of whom were Northern transplants. Three of us ordered the hard crabs as we locals call them (we say soft crabs too). One of my colleagues, a Midwesterner, after eating only two and neatly stacking the shells on a paper plate, was unable to eat any more because she said she had worked too hard for such a little bit of crab meat. Before this I had never thought about the efficiency or inefficiency of hard-crab pickin'.

I was raised in a place where people don't eat crabs, we feast on them. We sit for hours at long tables covered with newspaper in the middle of which are steaming mounds of Maryland's famous crustaceans. Each person is given a mallet and a knife to crack the orange-red shells. A good crab picker will remove every bit of the meat and even scrape out the yellowish fat in the corners of the shells to eat by itself or to add as flavoring to crab cakes. And if a crab claw is cracked just right, the meat comes out intact and the claw can be held by the pincers and dipped into a peppery vinegar mixture. In earlier days crab feasters would drink coffee, but today they prefer beer and Coca Cola.

Crabs are said to be fat, meaty and heavy, or poor, meager and light. They are given different names depending on their sex and stage of life: A male is a jimmie, a female a sook (pronounced *suk*) ; a paper shell is a soft crab turning into a hard crab; a buster is a crab shedding its hard shell; a peeler is about to begin the process of shedding.

In the 1950s and 1960s in Maryland, men would come around in trucks or old cars and sell housewives soft crabs and *feesh*. Cantaloupe-colored and perpetually in need of a shave, Bap, short for John Baptist, was one of those rowboat watermen. I remember his selling my mother cardboard flats of still-bubbling soft crabs covered with bits of seaweed. Mama would buy them and minutes later would be standing at the sink pitilessly cleaning them alive.

She was even more heartless when it came to the preparation of hard crabs. In one of his comedy routines Jeff Foxworthy talks about Louisiana in-laws who have to tell whatever they are steaming up to eat to get back in the pot. The Louisianans remind me of my own people. My mother would start out with a large kettle with a little water in it. She would then layer live crabs in the cooker, seasoning each layer generously (we like hard crabs salty and red hot with red pepper), placing a lid on the pot after the last layer was seasoned. As the water heated up the crabs started fighting and trying to climb over each other to get out. Mama would place bricks on the lid to keep them from escaping their terrible fate.

My mother sometimes made she crab but more often vegetable crab soup. When we would dish up some of that there would be a half a hard crab in the ladle. This soup and the cream of crab we liked as well were very spicy with cayenne, and so was Mama's deviled crab, a hotter version of the crab cake stuffed back in the shell and baked for a while.

Once good neighbors who often married each other, Virginians and Marylanders, though estranged today as a result of cultural cleansing, still enjoy the same seafood specialties. And the people in Southern Maryland and in the Northern Neck of Virginia have very similar holiday traditions. One Christmas season at an open house at Stratford Hall, birthplace of Robert E. Lee, I had not only General Lee's orange cake, but country ham and crab imperial that reminded me of my sister Ann's.

My Aunt Charlotte wins the award for soft crabs. Her recipe is simple: Dust crabs with flour and fry in a little clarified butter. Possibly the best restaurant crab cakes—and other traditional Chesapeake Bay dishes—are served at Hilda Crockett's on Tangier Island, Virginia (though I don't find the staff there as polite as I expect Virginians to be). The best homemade crab cakes I have ever eaten were prepared by my mother and by Mrs. P. W., a native of Calvert County, Maryland, from crabs harvested hardly any time before the cakes were patted out and fried.

Near my home in Clements, Maryland there are places that serve delicious crab cakes. One is actually a trailer that is pulled behind a pickup truck each day to the crossroads in Clements. Plastered with homemake signs advertising specials and regular menu items, this little crab house-on-wheels is operated by smiling ladies with Southern faces. They cook up what the men in their family catch in local estuaries. Real Marylanders, though we will eat Virginia or Carolina crab, prefer Maryland's. And under no circumstances will we knowingly eat Indonesian crab meat.

Diagonally across the intersection from the trailer is a plain little diner that serves crab cakes that are unsurpassed as far as their seasoning goes. They might or might not have been previously frozen; they may or may not contain a little filler—I never really cared if cakes had a few bread crumbs in them—but they have just the right amount of red pepper and very finely minced green pepper, which compliments the crab. Their crab cakes are fried on the grill, in the traditional way.

And excellent crab cakes can be had also at Mrs. Q.'s, a restaurant on the water just a few miles away from Clements. I don't notice many carpetbaggers at these little spots. They are too humble I think for the newcomers. At least there are still some places left where we can go to eat and visit and get away from Yankees for a while.

Hee Haw Redux

As residents of a border state, many Marylanders have found it advantageous to be Northern, given the ugly prejudices concerning the South. In a March 22, 2009 article in the *Washington Post Magazine*, Gene Weingarten, a native of—where else?—New York, writes that "no one can quite explain" why Maryland has a secessionist state song considering that "Maryland prefers its historical image as a Northern state, loyal to the Union."[1] He admits, however, that the truth is "a little less tidy." But the Marylander, the Southerner, really determined to pass for a Yankee need only talk that unpleasant Yankee talk, drive fast, act rude and never admit to liking country music. Though Northerners believe we listen exclusively to this genre, some of us in fact enjoy Vivaldi and Beethoven, Cole Porter and Gershwin. I like the music of Patti Page, Nat King Cole and the pop stars of the forties and fifties, and, though I may be thought "too plebeian," I even like those tacky cocktail lounge ballads such as "Fly Me to the Moon" and "Cry Me a River." Blissfully ignorant of current rock stars, nevertheless, I have been a fan of rock and roll from the era of Buddy Holly to the ascendancy of UB40. But, as any real Southerner, I have a weakness for country.

As an adolescent Anglophile decked out in mod fashions, I forswore "hillbilly" singers in the presence of carpetbagger classmates though

Maryland, My Maryland

I continued to listen to them secretly. Now when I openly admit an appreciation for the favorite music of the South, this always seems to elicit from carpetbaggers a gratuitous declaration of their taste for "classical" compositions by which they mean the selections—whether baroque, classical or "impressionist"—played by the strained-voiced pseudo-intellectuals on NPR.

But the country of Carrie Underwood and Jason Aldean hasn't much in common with mine and certainly not with the country of Hiram King "Hank" Williams or Ernest Tubb whose folksier style was gradually replaced beginning in the fifties by the less twangy music I heard on the kitchen Bakelite radio. And by the early sixties, I was listening to more "sophisticated" artists like Patsy Cline and Gentleman Jim Reeves.

As an unabashed lover of the country predating the twenty-first century (and conceding that some of it was depressing, sordid and just plain awful), I was naturally happy to have an opportunity to see Randy Travis in concert in 2002. Travis and vocalists like George Strait, Ricky Van Shelton and the tragic Keith Whitley were all part of a classic country revival spanning the 80s and 90s. With a surprising number of wonderful exceptions such as Josh Turner's "Long Black Train," most Music Row hits today are monotonic, lewd and uninspired. The country of contemporary artists is the studied, self-conscious country of the mall rat who has never known the desperation or poverty that inspired such songs as Merle Haggard's "If We Make It Through December." They are still played on some AM stations in Maryland—and Virginia—and it is good to hear that bare-feet-on-the-linoleum, hornet-on-the-back-porch country that my parents danced to at the Old Gum Tavern on Saturday nights.

In the 1940s when my mother was in high school, her Aunt Aggie and Aunt Helen would drive down to St. Mary's County from Washington D.C. where they had gone to work as nurses at St. Elizabeth's Hospital. After sunset the aunts and my mother's family would all pile into Helen's car and turn on the radio to listen to the *Grand Ole Opry*. The night air transmitted a clear signal, and my mother remembers what a joy it was for a young Maryland girl to hear the live performances from Nashville, Tennessee.

Once in a while famous country singers would make their way to Southern Maryland. My mother recalls the Carters' coming to St. Mary's County in the 1940s. In the 1960s Dolly Parton appeared at a concert at the local fairgrounds. My mother said that at the conclusion of her show, Dolly sat on the hay wagon talking casually to the fans and signing autographs, no one clamoring for her attention or crowding her. Southern Maryland people also frequented country music clubs such as Hotel Charles in Hughesville to see singers like Buck Owens and Roy Clark. Most often, though, we saw country artists on a black and white TV on Saturday evenings when we tuned in to programs such as the *Porter Wagoner Show*.

When I was a teen-aged cynic and wise in the ways of the world, I was above such rednecked diversions and ashamed of my parents' "'umble" rural ways. Today, however, when Yankees call me a hick for loving the music of the South, I am tempted to turn up the Loretta Lynn a little louder because, after all, "if you're looking at me, you're looking at country."

Maryland Is Hunt Country

Whether they live in Arkansas or Virginia, Mississippi or Maryland, Southern people love to hunt. Southerners go gunning for a variety of game—deer, wild boar, bear—but in the Upper Tidewater South the fox is the prey of legend. In Maryland the fox hunt has shaped society as much as the raising of tobacco or the harvesting of crabs and oysters.

Originally the sport of the Southern aristocrat, riding to hounds was the pastime of no less an historical figure than George Washington.[1] But it might have been the early Marylanders not the Virginians who introduced the hunt to the colonies.

> *In colonial days, the gentlemen of a neighbourhood would fore-gather in season for fox-hunting, which is believed to have taken*

its first hold in America in Tidewater Maryland. One early devotee of the sport, Robert Brooke, sailed out of England in 1650 with his family, a large retinue of servants and his pack of hounds and in that year established himself on the Patuxent River.[2]

In Maryland the hunt has typically been a social affair lasting for days. Proving that the state's reputation for Southern hospitality and culinary excellence was not unearned, one 1937 hunt breakfast menu includes "Maryland Rye Whiskey... Hot Apple Toddy...Roast Suckling Pig...Old Maryland Baked Ham...Brunswick Stew...Spoon Bread...Cornmeal Sticks."[3]

Hunting parties could traverse great distances, their hounds wandering so far afield they sometimes took a week getting back home. Speaking of an extraordinary hunt that predated the 1950s, an elderly St. Mary's County man recalled that it started in St. Mary's but ended only when a red fox had led the pack miles deep into neighboring Charles County. The same hunter swore that on one occasion after a dog had followed a fox into a hole the hound had backed out with the critter biting down on and still attached to his lip. From that day forward, the man said, the dog was given a special place by the fire to sleep.

There were two legendary huntsmen in St. Mary's County. Gray Fox Hayden, an unofficial hunt chieftain, knowing instinctively when it was time to give up a chase, would sing an old chant, the disappointed hunters joining in.

Come on boys and lets go home
And leave poor fox alone.
'Cause we've run him in the morning,
God knows!
We've run him in the evening,
God knows!
So come on boys and let's go home
And leave poor fox alone.

This chant had many other versions, but they are lost. Equally as celebrated was Irvy, his last name forgotten. Of African descent and a middle-aged man in the 1920s, he was preternaturally patient and was known to sneak up on rabbits and kill them with a knotty pine club which he would throw knocking them in the head. Irvy liked to entertain people with a recitation of a rhyme that would be considered scandalous today.

Fine winter morning,
N----- looking good,
Ax on his shoulder,
Heading for the wood.

What was most remarkable to the local population was Irvy's mysterious ability to lure dogs away from their masters. Owning no hounds himself, he would walk through town calling to them, and they would jump up from front porches and follow him.

By the 1950s in St. Mary's some people were resorting to chasing foxes in automobiles, my mother invited once to go on one of these hunts. When she heard about this, my paternal grandmother remarked, "Well you're in high society now." This more modern version of the hunt might or might not have been aristocratic, but whether riding to hounds on horseback or in Ford sedans, the fox hunter could be cruel, often allowing the hounds to worry—torture—a fox before they killed it. There were some people back then who had no stomach for this my mother told me.

Though I am afraid I would have been among those who would have left "poor fox alone," I am as fascinated with the romance of the hunt as anyone. And I have as any other Southerner a special affection for the hunting dog especially the hound be he blue tick, red bone or beagle. The Southerner gives his dog descriptive or whimsical names such as Big Paws, Loose Mouth, Annie and can identify a hound by its characteristic baying. In the 1950s a country lawyer, listening to his far-off pack and picking out the voice of his favorite, remarked to fellow hunters, "Ain't that pretty? Ain't that a pretty note?"

With the English setter or the pointer, men would go gunning for birds—bobwhite quail— on fall mornings in broom sedge fields. There was a lot of debating over the merits of different breeds of dogs relative to bird hunting: which was the "hard headed-est," which was most loyal, whose range was best suited to a particular hunt. These qualities were more important than any urbanite can begin to understand, and so much were the attributes of good dogs admired that one St. Mary's hunter was brought to tears by two setters on point, cutting eyes at each other just before breaking at exactly the same instant in pursuit of birds running on the ground.

The original bobwhite quail was fat and stupid. A huntsman expertly pumping a Model 12 Winchester at an ever-expanding circle of brown and white rising into the air could cut out two or three of the cock birds leaving the hens to assure a good hunt the next year. When the bobwhite quail was virtually wiped out by greedy "sportsmen," the natural resources people had to introduce its Mexican cousin, which proved smaller, smarter and faster and had a tendency to break up and go into the woods. The close-working English setter was best for hunting this new variety of game bird because, with his long coat, he was better protected than pointers in the brambles.

Bird was a traditional Christmas breakfast for some people in Southern Maryland. On Christmas morning, families would sit down to a platter of scrambled eggs circled by tiny butter-drenched quails. Another popular dish—anytime of year—was fried rabbit, which I have eaten but can't remember if I liked or not. And the little beagle was the dog for hunting this small game. For goose and duck hunting, however, Chesapeake Bay and black Labrador retrievers traditionally have been used. One of the latter breed, long cherished by Marylanders, was said to have accompanied the Second Maryland Infantry CSA as they charged up Culp's Hill. The Yankees deliberately shot the dog, but, to his credit, a Union commander issued an order for the burial of the Confederate mascot with full honors.

I had to "put down" my own black Lab a few years ago. Too stout for her skinny legs, she'd stick her nose out the window in the front room of our river shore home and sniff the air coming from the Virginia side when a storm was brewing. She had originally belonged to my son who had intended to make a hunting dog out of her, but she preferred eating potato chips by the hearth to retrieving ducks in freezing water.

My son, without a dog, hunts these days for Canada geese. He occasionally gets a deer, but my eldest granddaughter seems to get one more often (along with my son, she and her two younger siblings all routinely bring home prizes from turkey shoots). I do not hunt: I neither kill nor butcher. My contribution is fixing a respectable venison roast or goose smothered in mushroom gravy. I would much rather eat something killed swiftly, mercifully in the wild than some poor animal raised on a corporate farm.

The bond between Southerners and the natural world and God's creatures, the dogs that help us hunt and the game we both pursue, is a mystery to the outsider who looks with horror on hunting as primitive and proof of a lack of evolution when it is no more primal than eating or dancing. And discipline and beauty not only can be but must be imposed on natural inclinations. While I can't defend the inhumane aspects of riding to hounds, I have admiration and praise for the hunter who provides for his family.

GLOSSARY OF MARYLANDISMS

While I wish to emphasize that this sampling of Maryland regionalisms is not part of any formal linguistic study, I also believe that Marylanders are the only real authority on their own language. In compiling it I relied heavily on my co-natural knowledge of the speech of my people and input from fellow Southerners including Kentuckians. Because any effort to be precise about the way Marylanders say things is an exercise in futility, I have only approximated pronunciations in this glossary. And I have not resorted to the use of phonetic symbols because they are sometimes, I think, a distraction to the reader. I will leave them to the academics. The term *Maryland native* (MN) refers to anyone descended from the people who came voluntarily or otherwise to Maryland's shores in the seventeenth, eighteenth and early nineteenth centuries or from those who were living here when the first colonists arrived in 1634.

In my definitions and examples I have mentioned often the *Andy Griffith Show*, not because I am an admirer of the late Griffith or his politics, but because the producers and writers of his much-loved TV program made some attempt at authenticity. It is safe to assume that Griffith advised them on the expressions of his native North Carolina, many of which are found in Maryland as well. I have made also multiple references to the *Oxford English Dictionary* (OED) and to the novel *Gone with the Wind* (*GWTW*). Mitchell's characters are fictional, but their speech is real.

I hope that this glossary will be of value to those who love the South and its language and to those who might wish to investigate further the beautiful speech of Maryland.

a: Maryland natives use the broad *a*, as in *Baltimore*, when pronouncing *Talbot*, *Calvert* (though some Calvert Countians will disagree). They also use *a* to augment verbs for emphasis. George Washington employed this device. He writes in a journal that he "went a hunting again—found Nothing" (*Maryland's Way*, 169).

afeerd: Afraid. When my mother was a little girl, she heard an uncle, who had been badly burned in a house fire, say, "I'm afeerd to die."

amberlance/ambahlance: Ambulance. *Gone With the Wind's* Prissy pronounces the word "amberlance" (369). Maryland natives tend to use *ambahlance* stressing the first syllable and pronouncing the *a* in *lance* as the *a* in *ham*.

any: A. *Clear as any bell* translates into *clear as a bell*.

anyfeenk/anythink: Anything. There is a tendency among Marylanders in the remoter areas of the state to pronounce *th* as *f*, short *i* as *ee* and *g* as *k* just as some British do today. In spite of its tawdry story lines, the old BBC soap opera *EastEnders* is a gold mine of what is considered archaic language. Characters on the show often say *anyfeenk* and use other ancient forms found in the American South.

An eighty-six-year-old employee of London's most famous department store in an interview that aired on the Travel Channel (February 9, 2005) says, "You can get anythink you want [at Harrods]." The pronouncing of *g* as *k* has long been considered a bad habit by the keepers of "proper" speech. In *The Grand Repository of the English Language*, published in 1775, Thomas Spence writes, "Why should People be laughed at all their lives for betraying their vulgar education, when the Evil is so easily remedied? How ridiculous it is to hear People that can read saying 'Any Think'— 'A Horange'-'idear'" (Quoted in Brieg, *Colonial Williamsburg*, 82).

a plenty: Much or more than enough. Pork in *GWTW* tells Scarlett he has spilled "a plen'y" whiskey while fetching it in two hollowed-out gourds for Gerald O'Hara (405).

as: MNs and other Southerners (and Brits) might say, "Cold as it is, we had better bundle up." Northerners and speakers of "standard" English might say, "As cold as it is, we had better bundle up." The Northerner's intonation would also differ from ours, but it is beyond my ability to explain just how we in the South would render *cold as it is* or *hot as it is* or *crazy as he is!*

ast: Asked.

ax/axe: Ask. The *OED* quotes from an eleventh-century translation of John 21:12: "Nan Thaera...ne dorste hine axian hwaet he waere." This means *Now none (of the disciples)...dared ask, "Who are you?"* *OED* quotes from the Old English version of Matthew 22:46: "Ne man ne dorste hyne nan thing mare axiyean." This means *(Nor from that day) did anyone dare to ask him any more questions.* And *OED* tells us that in John Wyclif's 1368 translation of Luke 23:3, we will find: "Pilat axide hym, and seide, Art thou Kyng of Jewis?"

Axe is found in Chaucer's *Canterbury Tales*. The Wife of Bath, in her prologue, inquires, "I axe why the fyfte man was not housbond to the Samaritan?"

Because of metathesis speakers of English have tended to interchange letters adjacent to each other. For example, *wasp* started out life as *waps*. Over time, the *s* and the *p* were switched. *Bird* was actually *brid* long ago. *Grist* became the *grits* of today. The Old English *ascian* eventually became *acsian*. *Acsian/axian* survived in England as *ax/axe* until the 1600s. But *ask* gradually became standard. The colonists brought *ax* not *ask* with them, and it was preserved in the South, including Maryland, until present day. In Maryland *ax* is mainly in use today among those of African descent.

'bacca: Tobacco. The pronunciations *terbaccy* and *'baccy* are not Marylandisms.

bateau: dory-like, sea-worthy work boat used for oystering.

baughl: Boil. This is as close as I can come to representing the pronunciation of oi. In Maryland we heat our homes in winter with fuel aughl not with fuel oil.

beat: Pray or say. An aunt of mine told me that one summer evening when a severe storm was coming, a St. Mary's County man, addressing his wife, said, "Woman, beat those beads!" This can be translated into *Say your rosary fast because we are in peril*. When I was growing up, my family and other families in our community would gather in an interior room, pray and light blessed candles when black clouds approached.

bidawa: Biddie wire. This is chicken wire, particularly the specially coated chicken wire used in making crab pots.

bin: Been the verb or Ben the name.

bird: A peculiar, strong or otherwise remarkable personality. See *mess*. In a January 9, 1961 episode of *The Andy Griffith Show*, Andy, addressing his deputy, says, "Barney, you are a bird in this world."

bitter cold: Extraordinarily cold. Shakespeare uses the term in *Hamlet* (act 1, sc.1). A magazine editor once corrected my use of *bitter cold*—he changed it to *bitterly cold*. But the former implies a cold that penetrates body and spirit. *Bitterly cold* is a meteorological statement.

boo: I have always heard that a timid person wouldn't say boo. In finally coming to understand the strength of her sister-in-law, Scarlett O'Hara realizes too late how she has underestimated Melanie, having wrongly assumed that she had "lacked the courage to say Boo to a goose" (*GWTW*, 1000).

boogety, boogety, boogety: The meaning of this expression is not entirely certain. I once heard a NASCAR driver use it to describe a burst of speed. It is also heard in a folk song. When I was very young, a child would be bounced on a knee (as if riding an imaginary horse) while someone sang, "This is the way the ladies ride, ladies ride, ladies ride. This is the way the ladies ride so early in the morning." Then the bouncing would stop, and the person with the child on her knee would very slowly say, "Then 'long come the Boogey man and go...boogety, boogety, boogety!!" The *boogety* part is said quickly as the bouncing is suddenly resumed usually making the surprised child giggle.

booshal: Bushel, bushel basket. A *booshal* of crabs these days is worth a small fortune. My father used to ask me, "How many booshals do you love me?" I would reply with whatever number came to mind.

bother 'bout/botherin' 'bout: Desire, desiring. *He ain't botherin' 'bout sweetcorn today* means *he isn't desiring sweetcorn today*.

brag on: Praise highly a person or his accomplishments.

branch: Creek. People once liked to drink branch water and bourbon.

bugaboo: Boogey man. The word appears in the lyrics of this old song:

I fed my turkeys on dry peas.
I fed my turkeys on dry peas.
I fed my turkeys on dry peas.
Fust they laugh, and then they sneeze.
Walk your bones and a tucka too.
Never mind the bugaboo.
Walk your bones and a tucka too.
Never mind the bugaboo.

bullet rifle: Long gun with rifled barrel used in hunting and self-defense. The term *bullet rifle* is an example of Southern pleonasm as is the equally redundant *cut it half in two*.

butter won't melt in my mouth: I will not use harsh, critical words. Addressing Rhett Butler, Scarlett O'Hara says, "There's a time for all things. When I've got plenty of money, I'll be nice as you please, too. Butter won't melt in my mouth" (*GWTW*, 768).

care a mul: Caramel.

carry: Take. The title of the song "Carry Me Back to Old Virginny" is translated into *Take Me Back to Old Virginny*. *Carry* is also used as *take* in the spiritual "Swing Low, Sweet Chariot" in the line "coming for to carry me home." In the Southern Maryland of the 1940s, when a boy had a date with a girl, he did not take her out, he carried her out. To this day some Southern Marylanders still ask a neighbor or friend to carry them to church, to town. The term is used this way in North Carolina also.

chall: Child. Rarely heard today. A "reader" at my church says *chall*. She also pronounces *out oat*. When I see her standing at the lectern, I am always happy because she reads, and speaks, so beautifully.

chap: Child. The chapman in England was a seller of children's books.

(like a) chicken with its head cut off: Crazily. Anyone raised on a farm understands the meaning of this expression. Scarlett O'Hara's version is "chicken with its head off" (*GWTW*, 365-366).

chimbley: Chimney in parts of Maryland, Kentucky and England.

Christis: Belonging to Christ. *There wasn't neither Christis tomato left* means *there wasn't even one of Christ's tomatoes left.*

Christmas gift/gifts: Merry Christmas. This was still heard in St. Mary's County, Maryland in the 1960s. Irwin Russell's 1878 poem "Christmas-Night in the Quarters" begins, "When merry Christmas-day is done, And Christmas-night is just begun; While clouds in slow procession drift, To wish the moon-man 'Christmas gift'..." (Young, *Southern Treasury,* 91).

common: Ill bred, dishonest, violent or obscene. See *ordinary*. Someone can be said to act common. When a person curses or makes reference to the scatological, he has a common mouth on him. And if somebody does you common, he does not treat you fairly. Expecting bad weather, old time Marylanders would say that it was going to do common. Mammy tells Scarlett that "it was downright common" of her to have had an easy time during childbirth, in this case using the word to mean ill bred, lower class (*GWTW,* 135). Scarlett calls Emmie Slattery "an overdressed, common, nasty piece of poor white trash" (*GWTW,* 528).

cooper: Pronounced—and this is only a rough approximation—*cuppa*. A Southern surname. Also, *broom* is pronounced *brum* and *room rum*.

countian: A person from a county.

crease/ creese(s): Cress. *OED* says *crease* or *creese(s)* has been used for over a thousand years to mean *bitter field greens* especially the nasturtium species. *OED* also says that *cress* is an obsolete form of *crease*, meaning *to fold*. Older speakers in Maryland say *watercrease, watercreazy, wintercrease* or *wintercreazy* for *watercress*. It is a popular green in the South and grows wild. I remember eating it seasoned with fat meat. It was also long, long ago an important ingredient in St. Mary's County stuffed ham.

curl up: Take offense at something or someone.

cut: Turn. Southern people cut the lights on and off. Also dance, as in these lines from an old song: "Tied my horse to the swingin' limb; my horse cut the pigeon wing."

cut some shines: Act mischievously, vigorously or violently.

dasn't: Dare not. My distant cousin Teensy Hayden Alvey used this expression often. She would say, "I dasn't (do this or that)." *Dasn't* is heard in Kentucky, I am told by a native of the Blue Grass State, and in some areas of London, according to an Eastender I know.

dead man's fingers/dead men: The gills of a crab. Clarissa Dickson Wright and Jennifer Paterson of BBC's *Two Fat Ladies*, a popular 1990s cooking show, use this term.

'deed: Indeed. Replying to the statement, "It's certainly cold today," a Marylander would say "'Deed it is, Cap'n."

deesh: Dish in St. Mary's County, Maryland and on Maryland's Eastern Shore.

doll baby: Doll or baby doll. Also a term of endearment. In his *Letters from Lee's Army*, Virginian Charles Minor Blackford writes:

During the evening as I was riding over part of the field where there were many dead yankees lying who had been killed...I noticed an old doll-baby with only one leg lying by the side of a Federal soldier just as it dropped from his pocket when he fell writhing in the agony of death. It was obviously a memento of some little loved one at home which he had brought so far with him and had worn close to his heart...I dismounted, picked it up and stuffed it back into the poor fellow's cold bosom that it might rest with him in the... grave (33).

done: Has. *He done left me* means *he has left me.*

draf denn: Pronounced *droff den*. A wooded area in which livestock graze. *A Concise Anglo-Saxon Dictionary* defines *draf* as a "road along which cattle are driven," and *denn* as a "swine-pasture."[1]

dreen: Drain.

drownded: Drowned.

dug/doag: Dog. See *hug/hoag*. This pronunciation is heard in St. Mary's County and Westmoreland County, Virginia. A similar pronunciation can be heard in the cowboy's *little doggies*.

Dog whichever way it is pronounced figures into several Maryland expressions. *Dog, dog out* mean *wear out*. *To put on the dog* means *to put on airs, to be pretentious*. Someone who is very ill is sick as a dog, and if you treat a person "like" a dog you are abusive towards him.

dung'l/dung'l 'ens: Dung hill, dung hill hens. The original organic, free-range chickens were dung hill hens who scratched in the barnyard for worms and grubs.

eel: Ill. Pronounced this way in St. Mary's County until the 1950s, according to my mother.

either/either other: A single. If someone says that he didn't catch either fish or either other fish, he caught no fish at all. See *neither*.

'er/up 'er: There, up there. A distant kinsman of mine uses *up 'er* for *up there*. A Baltimore native I know also pronounces *there 'er*.

evil: Mean. Someone can be said to be evil as a black snake. Black snakes are known to be aggressive.

fall out/fell out: Have an argument (a falling out), had an argument. People often fall out over politics and religion.

far: Fire.

feist: A little yapping dog.

flug gum: Homemade box traps.

foolin'with: Bothering with, caring for. Scarlett O'Hara says, "Maybe I'll learn about babies sometime…but I'm never going to like fooling with them" (*GWTW*, 144).

for: In order. When it is used with an infinitive, it indicates the object of an action as in *for to carry me home*. In *Lanfranc's Chirurgie* (c. 1400) we find, "For to clense the wounde use the medicyn of mel roset" (*OED*). And George Washington, in a journal entry dated April 8, 1748, writes, "You must ride round the back of the Mountain for to get below them" (*OED*). The French also use *for* (*pour*) preceding an infinitive.

gane: Gone. Clarissa Dickson Wright, one of BBC's *Two Fat Ladies*, distinctly pronounces *o* as a long *a*, *coconut cake-a-nut*, *no nay*, *toasted tasted*. See *phane*.

Gawd: God. Mammy exclaims, "'Bress (bless) Gawd." in *GWTW* (987). The Eastenders of London pronounce *God Gawd*. Archie Bunker's pronunciation of the word *God* is not the same, however.

goloshes: Galoshes. A type of boot. This is how my father pronounced the word, placing the emphasis on the first syllable.

good old boy: A regular fellow. The British say this too. David Dickinson, host of the BBC program *Bargain Hunt*, uses *good old boy* in an episode that aired on March 26, 2005.

grue: To feel terror or horror. It also means to shudder, tremble or quake. The word comes from Northern England and Scotland according to *OED*.

having a time: Having fun or having difficulty doing something. A high school French teacher of mine, from Chicago, made fun of our using this expression.

heah: Here. But we pronounce the *ah* only lightly.

hit: Done. See *lick*.

hoase: House. See "Saving Maryland's Southern Speech."

hollerin' about: Calling for or talking about. *They are hollerin' about snow tomorrow* means *they are predicting snow*.

hongry: Hungry. Dilcey in *GWTW* says, "Nuthin' wrong wid dis child cept he hongry" (408).

hound dog: Hound. Another Southern pleonasm.

house: In Maryland and Kentucky, a transitive verb meaning to hang tobacco in a barn. The *s* in this word is pronounced as a *z*. The *OED* says *house* means "to keep or store in a house or building." *Housing tobacco* is used interchangeably with *putting up tobacco*. In September of 2006, a friend of mine heard a farmer in a waffle house in Eastern Kentucky talk about housing tobacco.

house burn: A form of damage to curing tobacco. Heard in Kentucky and Maryland.

howsumever/howsomever: Howsoever. *Howsome'er* is found in Shakespeare (*All's Well*, act 1, sc. 3).

hug/hoag: Hog. My great aunt Hope Thompson Adams pronounced *hog* this way, although precisely how she said the word is impossible to duplicate. *Hogshead* is pronounced

lick: A little work. A tong full. *He ain't hit (done) a lick* means *he ain't done much work*. Maryland watermen call what they bring up from the water each time they throw and close tongs a *lick*. They strike a lick.

lightnin' bug: Firefly to the Northerner, the term is heard in Maryland and Kentucky.

loggy: Pronounced "loagy." Like a log. Tired and plodding.

make you cuss your grandmother: Delicious!

make you swallow your tongue: Delicious!

manapoorsha/manapoasha: Two of the many variations on and corruptions of *mania a potu* or *mania potu*. In *The Principles and Practice of Medicine* (1918), Sir William Osler writes, "Delirium tremens (mania a potu), an incident in the history of chronic alcoholism, results from the long-continued action of the poison on the brain."[2] *Mania a potu* is a Latin phrase. *Potu*, I am told by a scholar friend, is the ablative of the Latin noun *potus* meaning *drink*. Here the ablative case indicates a cause and effect relationship so *mania a potu* means, literally, *the madness caused by drink* or *the madness of drink*. Jon Neill, MD and Francis Gurney Smith, MD tell us in *An Analytical Compendium of the Various Branches of Medical Science*, published in 1856, that *mania a potu*, that is *delirium tremen* or *delirim c. tremore*, is "the brain fever of drunkards." A patient suffering from this syndrome "is perpetually haunted by frightful creatures."[3]

Mania a potu has been corrupted to *manapoorsha/manapoasha* and has come to mean *an alcoholic binge*. A "binger" might, for example, go on a three-week *manapoorsha*. But older people speak of a *manapoorsha* as though it were something greatly to be feared. They consider it a state of insanity caused by excessive consumption of alcohol. Someone can drink so much that he has gone into fits. I am convinced that *manapoorsha* is a corruption of *mania a potu* since both the meaning and the pronunciation are too similar to ascribe to chance.

Dr. John Roache of St. Mary's County brought this word to my attention.

mannish: Manly. *OED* defines mannish as "of a woman, her attributes, etc.: Resembling a man, man-like, masculine. Chiefly contemptuous." My mother would often tell me when I was not acting properly to stop being mannish.

mawmaw: Mama or grandmother.

mess: A sufficient or more than sufficient number or amount of. Southerners catch a mess of fish and cook a mess of greens (kale, collard, turnip greens). We instinctively know how much or how many are in a mess. The word also denotes a singularly peculiar, eccentric, endearing or interesting personality. *That girl is a mess* could be applied to a cute but mischievous child. *Mess* can also mean a scandal.

Miss Agnes/Lordy Miss Agnes: Goodness gracious! My father said this. In an *Andy Griffith Show* episode that aired on November 15, 1965, Andy exclaims, "Miss Agnes!"

mister man: One "having a certain occupation," a man "of all classes" (*OED*). It "survives dialectally in Yorkshire" (*OED*). It also survives today in Maryland.

mother wit: Craftiness, wiliness.

murry: Merry

Name of God/Name of the Lord: Scarlett O'Hara begs, "Name of God, Doctor! Please!" when she learns a physician isn't leaving wounded soldiers to tend to Melanie (*GWTW*, 357).

nary: Not, not a. *He caught nary a fish* and *he caught nary fish* mean *he didn't catch any fish.*

neither: A single. He didn't catch neither fish. See *either.*

note/noting: Give, giving off an odor.

oat: Out.

of: Follows *taste, feel, smell.* In Daniel Defoe's *Robinson Crusoe* (1719), we find "She went to it, smelled of it, and ate it" (*OED*).

oncet/twicet: Once, twice.

onliest: Only.

ordinary: Low class, unrefined but not necessarily poor. See *common.* South of the Mason-Dixon Line, wealth or the lack of wealth is not an indicator of class. When I was growing up in relative poverty much of the time, my mother would say about certain folks that they were "really very ordinary." I would know exactly what kind of people she was describing without knowing anything else about them, but a lack of resources did not bear on the quality of being ordinary.

pallet: Layers of blankets, quilts, etc. spread out on the floor on which overnight guests sleep. The term is used in *GWTW* (132, 448).

patteroll/patterollers: Groups of horsemen including Union cavalrymen who at various times terrorized people in the South. An elderly black man from Charles County, Maryland told us that when he was a little boy, he was warned that the patterollers would get him if he misbehaved. Jeems in *GWTW* (23) talks about being caught by the "patterollers."

phane: Phone. I once heard a Yankee ridicule a young Maryland girl's British pronunciation of this word. See *gane*.

playshoar: Pleasure. Pronounced this way on Maryland's Eastern Shore.

poke: Sack or bag. It is used in the expressions *pig in a poke, possum in a poke*. *Southern Living's Cooking Across the South* includes a recipe for poke "sallet," a wild green so named because people would pick it and put it in a poke. My mother often prepared poke salad. I remember also a popular rock and roll song in the early 1960s called "Poke Salad Annie."

poor's house: Poor house. *Poor's* (as used here) is a fossilized form of the Old English genitive (possessive) case. It is a vestige of the inflections found in early languages like Saxon, Latin and Classical Greek.

pot likker: Water in which greens are cooked.

pulling faces: Making faces. In *GWTW* (442) Mama Fontaine, who is oddly blunt for a Southern lady, after saying something "scandalous," tells her daughter-in-law, "Don't pull such a shocked face Jane."

rag: Cloth as in dish rag, wash rag.

rag rug: A rug made from braided strips of rags sewn together into an oval or round shape. See *GWTW*, 461.

rare: Foul. When someone is in a bad mood, he is in a rare mood.

ready: Outrageous, difficult, one of a kind, rough and tumble. *He's ready* means *he's a mess* or *he's really something*. I once heard a real Floridian (rarer than a real Marylander) use *ready* in this way.

reckon: Contrary to what Yankees think, *reckon* is a perfectly respectable and useful word. It is very Southern and very British, and every true Marylander should be proud to use it regardless of Northern ignorance. My Uncle Woodrow often said, "I reckon."

reeplace: Correct Southern/British pronunciation of the word *replace*. In an episode of the 1990s BBC America show *House Invaders*, Linda Barker, an interior designer, pronounces *replace* this way.

right: Very. Used today by Southerners and the British as a modifier of adjectives but not by speakers of "American" except in titles such as *the right reverend* and *the right honorable*. Shakespeare's Hamlet uses the term *right well*. *He ain't right* is a Maryland expression that means *he is crazy*. *Now you know he's right!* means *you certainly know he is a strong, remarkable or outrageous personality*.

right smart: Quite a bit, too much. *That's right smart of money to pay* means *that is too much money to pay*. *Right smart* is also used for *very*. *It's right smart humid today* means *it's very humid today*.

row skiff: A row boat.

run mad: Frantic, hurried. The term is found in Mary Chestnut's *A Diary from Dixie* (54).

s: The Southern *s* is pronounced as a *z*. See *zinc*. The correct Southern spelling of *realize* is *realise*.

severe: Fierce, extraordinary, imposing on your sensibilities with great force.

shivered/shivering: Shattered, shattering. Scarlett O'Hara (*GWTW* 368) thinks that the Yankees are attacking Atlanta because the ground is shaking and window glass has "shivered" and fallen in sharks everywhere. A little later Scarlet learns from Prissy that the "nerve-shivering sounds" were only Confederate armaments exploding as they were being destroyed to keep them from the enemy in the event the Yankees took the town (369). In the 1980s I heard a Maryland native use *shivered* in the same sense.

shypoke: An earthy, colonial Maryland term for a marsh hen, a type of river shore bird.

slow along: Go along slowly.

snake doctor: Agnes Swales, of African descent, in the 1950s took care of my siblings and me. She would sometimes raise my baby brother Paul up in the air, kiss his face and call him snake doctor, laughing the whole time. Agnes had no idea how old she was when she worked for my mother and father, but my guess is sixty or older. *Snake doctor* was, apparently, a term of endearment. It also means *dragonfly*.

snap beans: String or green beans.

snay-w: Snow (approximate Maryland/Australian pronunciation).

souse/ soused: A jellied luncheon meat made with pig knuckles and pig's feet. Also a verb meaning *pickled* and an adjective meaning *drunk*. In *GWTW* (461) *soused* is used to mean *wet*.

Southern Maryland: The lowest counties of Maryland's Western Shore. The term should always be capitalized. Southern Maryland is not to be confused with the Eastern Shore which is on the east side of the Chesapeake Bay.

spring of the year/fall of the year: Spring, fall.

squz/squooze: Squeezed. Someone in Maryland or Kentucky might say, "I *squz* all the water out of the sponge."

started: Startled. The hunter started a rabbit.

sure enough: Certainly, indeed it is so. My mother heard *sure enough* often when she was a child. I had believed, incorrectly, that this expression was not used in Maryland, but now I know it is just one more Southernism lost to us.

swan: Swear. This is heard in Maryland and Kentucky.

(well I) swear at Mollie: Goodness gracious.

taa taa: Pronounced with the flat *a* of *apple*, *taa*, according to *OED*, is "an infantile word expressing thanks." I remember saying taa taa to babies and toddlers to coax from them something they held in their hands.

tea: Real Southern tea is by definition a beverage that is very sweet and served cold. The *sweet* in *sweet tea* is therefore redundant. When I was a teenager, one of my jobs was preparing the tea for supper, and I always added lots of sugar to the pitcher containing the still-warm brew. Because of the influx of Yankees to Maryland, few restaurants here serve tea Southern style anymore.

tea towel: Dish towel. The Irish use this term also.

thee: You. *Thee* was used by some St. Mary's Countians way back my mother says. And it is heard among the people in Devonshire I am told but cannot confirm. Further, it is also heard in Yorkshire as documented in the James Herriot books about the life of a country veterinarian in that region.

th-hee-eighta: My father's pronunciation of *theater*.

thow/thew: Throw, threw. I remember someone's correcting one of my brothers when he pronounced *throw thow*, telling him that he sounded "ignorant." The irony is that the person who was "enlightening" my brother was the ignorant one. *Thow* and *thew* are proper Southern pronunciations. Some Brits also pronounce the words this way.

tire: Tier. Newly cut and speared tobacco is hung from *tire* poles in barns to cure.

'tis: It is. My Uncle Woodrow used this contraction.

tore 'em up: Was extraordinarily successful in an endeavor or enterprise. Someone once said of a hunter who shot many rabbits, "By Christ he tore 'em up."

tore up: Intoxicated. *I got tore up Saturday night* means I *got drunk*.

tow: Very blond, almost white haired. Emmie Slattery in *GWTW* (527) is described as a "dirty tow-headed slut."

tuther: The other as in *it will rain or snow, one or tuther*. See *GWTW*, 527.

water dog: Refers usually to a retriever. It is also a general term that is applied to a dog that swims well and is at home in the water.

ways on him/her: *He has his ways on him* means *he is being unpleasant*.

well: Here I am or what may I do for you?

wif/weef: With. This is heard among London's Eastenders.

worry: Bother. I have often heard Marylanders say something or someone worried them to death. Years ago *worry* meant *to tear and rip and pull*. A dog was said to worry a possum, for example, that is to shake the possum violently. Dubose Heyward in his novel *Porgy* describes a hurricane ravishing Charleston, South Carolina: "Notch by notch the velocity increased. The concussions upon the roofs became louder, and the prying fingers commenced to gain a purchase, worrying small holes into larger ones" (Young, *Southern Treasury*, 718).

yew: You. Lucy Davis, an English actress who played Dawn in the BBC's *The Office* pronounces *you* this way. She was born in Warwickshire. She also pronounces *acting actink*.

yonder: There. It is found in Shakespeare. My mother said many people used this expression when she was a child. When I attended Father Andrew White School in the fifties, a classmate said to me, "Look over yonder." Even at my young age, I had been robbed of my pure Southern dialect, and I remember thinking the girl had said something that "people" just weren't suppose to say. A few years earlier, before the world found its way to St. Mary's, her Shakespearean language would have gone unnoticed. There is, however, little of Shakespeare left in the Mother County these days. And not much left of him down yonder in the rest of the South for that matter.

your own self: Yourself. Sheriff Andy Taylor says to Barney, "You should be excited your own self."

zinc: Sink.

zounds: Corruption of God's Wounds. This expression fossilizes the ancient pronunciation of *s* and the pre-vowel shift pronunciation of *ou*. In the 1930s in St. Mary's County, *zounds* was a favorite expression of Cora Wilson, who was born in bondage. A strict observer of decorum, tall and angular and "so black she was purple," she drank gin and smoked a corncob pipe.

The Reflexive Dative

I purchased me a dress and *get you another biscuit* are not incorrect. Only Yankees think that the use of the reflexive dative is backwards.

Joyce Bennett

Subject-Verb Agreement

In the South in days past the rules about subject-verb agreement differed from those of today, and Southerners of all social classes at one time said, "He don't." One morning, when my father was very young, his family was enjoying some salt fish (dried, salted shad or herring, traditionally drenched in white cornmeal and fried in lard, a dish popular in Tidewater Maryland and Virginia). My father, whose family was poor, remembered being happy to be having such a feast. But a neighbor just dropping by, observing the salt fish breakfast, remarked, "I sees other people lives hard too." The early-morning caller was not of African descent. I point this out because it is important to note that culturally intact black people have preserved that neighbor's now-archaic syntax.

Terms of Respect/Affection

Those unschooled in Southern English consider racist the practice of calling an elderly black person *aunt* or *uncle*, but in the South until recently this was considered polite. Older, well-respected members of Southern society, regardless of race, were addressed in this manner. Applying familial terms to those who are not kin is a way to show deference. Also a Southernism is calling a younger man of any race *son*.

Southern fathers refer to the eldest female child as *daughter*. There are several other terms of affection heard only occasionally today, terms such as *sissy, little sis, sis, brother, bubba,* buddy, *mama/momma, daddy* (used by all ages), *granddaddy, grand pop, pop, granny, grandmomma, grandmother. Grandma* and *grandpa* were not used until more recently. *Mom* and *dad*, irritating Yankeeisms, are replacing the more traditional *mama/momma* and *daddy*. But even *daddy* was once considered too modern and disrespectful; *papa* was preferred.

Also too modern and disrespectful in the 1920s in Maryland was calling a husband by his given name alone. The first time my maternal grandmother referred to my grandfather as Tom rather than Mr. Tom they had been married for a while, and she was so embarrassed at the familiarity she put her hands over her ears. And lest feminists take offense at this, they should know that Southern husbands, genuinely respectful of womankind, would call their wives Miss Rose or Miss Mary Alice.

NOTES

PRELUDE

1. Jefferson Davis, *The Rise and Fall of the Confederate Government* (New York: D. Appleton and Company, 1881), 1:337.

GEOGRAPHY

Shrinking the South

1. *St. Mary's Beacon*, October 25, 1860.
2. Ibid., April 18, 1861.
3. *Mitchell's Primary Geography* (Philadelphia: E. H. Butler & Co., 1864), 54-55.
4. "The Confederate Cause in Maryland," *Confederate Veteran*, January 1894, 9.
5. Lt. Shepherd Green Pryor to Penelope Pryor, February 23, 1862, McDowell, Virginia. Transcription of letter written from Camp Allegheny appears on interpretive sign at McDowell Battlefield.
6. Becky Kellogg, "Tornado Expert Ranks Top Tornado States," http://www.weather.com/outlook/weather-news/news/articles/top-tornado-states_2012-03-06.

Changes in Latitude: More on Southern Geography

No annotation.

Joyce Bennett

A HISTORY UNRECONSTRUCTED

Maryland State Song Under Attack—Again and Again

1. Anne Christmas, "Maryland Song Nears 100," *Evening Star,* December 31, 1960.
2. Lori Montgomery, "Teen Leads New Quest to Drop Md. Song; Assembly Revisits Lyrics Debate," *Washington Post*, March 5, 2001, http://pqasb.pqarchiver.com/washingtonpost/access/69225128.html?FMT=FT&pf=1 md state song article.
3. Ibid.
4. Sam Francis, "Abolishing America (contd.): State Songs Under P.C. Attack…," Creators Syndicate, Inc., March 15, 2001, http://www.vdare.com/articles/abolishing-america-contd-state-songs-under-pc-attack.

My Hometown: A Rank Secession Hole

1. S.C.A., "Feasting in St. Mary's," *Baltimore Sun,* May 19, 1910, 11.
2. "Found Eldorado in an Old Maryland Town and Didn't Know It," *Washington Post,* December 16, 1906, A4.
3. Linda Reno, "The Story of Abraham Barnes," St. Mary's Families, July 2001, http://userpages.umbc.edu/~pdavis2/Participants/dawsonm/smc/articles_files/july_ABarnes.html.
4. Aleck Loker, *A Most Convenient Place: Leonardtown, Maryland 1650-1950* (Leonardtown, MD: The Commissioners of Leonardtown and Solitude Press, 2001), 45.
5. Frederick L. McCoy, "Steamboat Days," Letter from St. Gabriel's Manor, *The Chesapeake,* November 2010, 10-11.
6. J.B Couch, e-mail message to author, November 18, 2010.
7. *St. Mary's Beacon*, August 8, 1861.

Maryland's Revised History: A Tangled Web

1. Carter T. Gray, introduction to *Postcard History Series, Calvert County* (Mount Pleasant, SC: Arcadia Publishing, 2000).

Maryland History by the Numbers

1. Wayde Chrismer, "The Emmitsburg Area in the Civil War," pt.2, Emmitsburg Area Historical Society Website, www.emmitsburg.net/archive_list/articles/history/civil_war/wayde?chrismer_civil_war_2.html.
2. James M. McPherson, *Ordeal by Fire: The Civil War and Reconstruction* (New York: Alfred A. Knopf, 1982), 358.
3. Raphael Semmes, *Memoirs of Service Afloat During the War Between the States* (Baltimore: Kelly, Piet & Co., 1869), 398-399.
4. Mary Chestnut, *A Diary from Dixie,* facsimile of 1905 ed. (New York: Gramercy Books, 1997), 188.
5. Lawrence M. Denton, *A Southern Star for Maryland* (Baltimore: Publishing Concepts, 1995), 180.
6. Bart Rhett Talbert, *Maryland: The South's First Casualty* (Berryville, VA: Rockbridge Publishing Company, 1995), 95.
7. McPherson, 152.

The 1860 Presidential Election in Maryland

1. John T. Willis, *Presidential Elections in Maryland* (Mt. Airy, MD: Lomond Publications, Incorporated., 1984), 177.
2. Francis Butler Simkins and Charles Pierce Roland, *A History of the South,* 4th ed. (New York: Alfred A. Knopf, Inc., 1972), 203-204.
3. John Thomas Scharf, *History of Maryland from the Earliest Period to the Present Day* (Baltimore: John B. Piet, 1879), 3: 463n, 463.
4. Abraham Lincoln to A.W. Bradford, November 2, 1863, in Scharf, 563.

5. Scharf. 587-589.
6. Willis, 52.
7. Scharf, 559.
8. Ibid., 570n1.
9. "Historical Election Results," U.S. Electoral College webpage, U.S. National Archives and Records Administration Website, http://www.archives.gov/federal-register/electoral college/historical.html.

Trail of Lies

1. There is a legend that after the battles of Chancellorsville and the Wilderness, the people of St. Mary's County, Maryland noticed an absence of turkey buzzards in their area. This was attributed to the mass migration of these morbid scavengers as they sought "carrion men, groaning for burial."

Onderdonkian History

1. "University of Maryland Presidents, 1859-Present," University of Maryland website, http://www.president.umd.edu/pastpres/onderdonk.
2. Henry Onderdonk, *History of Maryland from Its Settlement, to 1877* (Baltimore: John Murphy & Co., 1879), 261.
3. A Marylander, *Dulany's History of Maryland from 1632 to 1881* (Baltimore: Wm. J. C. Dulany and Company, 1881), 279.

Barbara Fritchie and Stonewall Jackson

1. Also spelled Frietchie.
2. Suzanne Ellery Chapelle, *The Maryland Adventure* (Layton, UT: Gibbs Smith, 2005), 114.
3. Ibid., 119-120.
4. Charles T. Duvall, *The Maryland Scene* (Baltimore: Remington Putnam Book Co., 1943), 112.

5. John Greenleaf Whittier, letter to the editor, *Century Illustrated Monthly Magazine* 32 (1886): 783.
6. Henry Kyd Douglas, *I Rode with Stonewall*, endnotes by Fletcher M. Green (St. Simons Island, GA: Mockingbird Books, Inc., 1989), 152.
7. Fletcher M. Green, endnotes to Douglas, 348n4.
8. Duvall, 111.
9. Larry Fox, "Frederick, Past Present," *Washington Post*, Friday, June 30, 1995, N06.
10. Scharf, *History of Maryland*, 442-443.

THE SOUTHERN PERSPECTIVE ON MARYLAND

Introduction

1. Anna Caroline Benning, "Review of the Histories Used in Southern Schools and Southern Homes," *Confederate Veteran*, December 1902, 550.
2. Belle Kearney, *A Slaveholder's Daughter* (New York: The Abbey Press, 1900; *Documenting the American South*, 1997) chap. 11, 113, http://docsouth.unc.edu/fpn/kearney/kearney.html. Citations are to online edition.
3. Ibid., chap. 18, 184.
4. Davis, *Rise and Fall*, 330.

Mary Chestnut

1. Chestnut, *Diary from Dixie*, 383.

Robert E. Lee and the Liberation of Maryland

1. A.L. Long, *Memoirs of Robert E. Lee* (Edison, NJ: The Blue and Grey Press, 1983), 206.
2. Ibid., 207-209.

3. Susan Leigh Blackford and Charles Minor Blackford, *Letters from Lee's Army*, ed. Charles Minor Blackford III (Lincoln, NE: University of Nebraska Press, 1998), 226.
4. Scharf, *History of Maryland*, 498.
5. Personne, dispatches to *Charleston Mercury*, September 7, 1862 and September 8, 1862, quoted in Sharf, 496-497.
6. Douglas, *I Rode with Stonewall*, 149.
7. Chestnut, *A Diary from Dixie*, 292-293.

The Angel of Chimborazo

1. Phoebe Yates Pember, *A Southern Woman's Story* (St. Simons Island, GA: Mockingbird Books, Inc., 1987), 44.

MARYLANDERS IN THE WAR

Governor Hicks: Accidental Defender of Maryland History

1. *St. Mary's Beacon*, Dec. 12, 1861.
2. CIVIS, letter to the editor, *St. Mary's Beacon*, January 3, 1861. This writer also refers to Unionist sentiment in Texas. The governor there having refused to call a special session of the legislature, the people of the state proceeded without him to settle the question of secession. Maryland lawmakers proved too conservative allowing Lincoln the time he needed to occupy their state. In order for Maryland constitutionally to have taken up the question of secession, the governor was required to call first a special session of the legislature, which would vote on a sovereign convention to which delegates would be sent by the people. At this convention, secession would be voted up or down. Hicks, as his letter of December 1861 confirms, feared that Maryland would secede and waited until the state was occupied by Northern troops before calling a special session. CIVIS writes that Maryland was "drifting into a sea of trouble,

without compass, pilot, or captain, saving and excepting an old woman in petticoats for a Governor."
3. *St. Mary's Beacon*, December 6, 1860.
4. Davis, *Rise and Fall*, 330.
5. Talbert, *South's First Casualty*, 41.
6. *St. Mary's Beacon*, Dec. 12, 1861.
7. Davis, *Rise and Fall*, 337.
8. Bradley T. Johnson, "Maryland," in *Confederate Military History*, ed. Clement A. Evans, vol. 2 (Atlanta: Confederate Publishing Co., 1899), 16.
9. Editorial, *St. Mary's Beacon*, May 9, 1861.

What Dr. Mudd Saw

No annotation.

Confederate Rose

1. Chestnut, *Diary from Dixie*, 176.
2. Rose O'Neal Greenhow, *My Imprisonment and the First Year of Abolition Rule at Washington* (London: Richard Bentley, Publisher in Ordinary to Her Majesty, 1863; *Documenting the American South*, 1998), chap. 4, http://docsouth.unc.edu/fpn/greenhow/greenhow.html. Citation is to online edition.
3. William Saffire, underbook, including sources and commentary, *Freedom* (New York: Avon Books, 1988), 1257, 1291.
4. Ishbel Ross, *Rebel Rose: Life of Rose O'Neal Greenhow, Confederate Spy* (New York: Harper & Brothers, 1954), 265.

Lamb to the Slaughter?

1. Elizabeth Steger Trindal, *Mary Surratt: An American Tragedy* (Gretna, LA: Pelican Publishing Company, Inc., 1996), 129-130.

2. Louis J. Weichmann, *A True History of the Assassination of Abraham Lincoln and of the Conspiracy of 1865*, ed. Floyd E. Risvold (New York: Vintage Books, 1977), 265.
3. Ibid., 11-12.

Who Was John Wilkes Booth?

1. Samuel Bland Arnold, *Memoirs of a Lincoln Conspirator*, ed. Michael W. Kauffman (Bowie, MD: Heritage Books, Inc., 2003), 49.
2. Ibid., 42.
3. John Wilkes Booth, November 1864, in *Daily National Intelligencer*, April 20, 1865.

MARYLAND: HEART AND SOUL OF THE CONFEDERATE NAVY

Admiral Semmes: Southern Born, Southern Bred

1. Semmes, *Service Afloat*, 468.
2. John M. Taylor, *Confederate Raider: Raphael Semmes of the Alabama* (Washington: Brassey's Inc., 1994), 259.
3. Warren F. Spencer, *Raphael Semmes: The Philosophical Mariner* (Tuscaloosa: The University of Alabama Press, 1997), 119, 154, 231.
4. Semmes, 453.
5. Ibid., 579.
6. Ibid., 167-169.
7. Taylor, 277.
8. Ibid., 273
9. Spencer, 123.
10. Taylor, 276.
11. Ibid., 44.
12. Semmes, 37-38.
13. Taylor, 123.
14. Semmes, 355.

15. Taylor, 252-253.
16. Semmes, 578.
17. Taylor, 45, 219.
18. Ibid., 42.
19. Spencer, 163.
20. Semmes, 110.
21. Taylor, 276.
22. Semmes, 801.

Admiral Franklin Buchanan: Reluctant Confederate?

1. Buchanan to George Buchanan Coale, May 29, 1861, in Charles Lee Lewis, *Admiral Franklin Buchanan: Fearless Man of Action* (Baltimore: The Norman, Remington Company, 1929), 165.
2. Buchanan, letter to the editor, *Richmond Examiner*, May 18, 1862, in Lewis, 168.
3. Ibid.
4. Buchanan to George Buchanan Coale, in Lewis, 166-167.
5. Buchanan, letter to the editor, *Examiner*, in Lewis, 169.
6. Buchanan to Coale, in Lewis, 167.
7. Buchanan, letter to the editor, *Examiner*, in Lewis, 168.
8. Buchanan to Coale, in Lewis, 167.
9. Ibid., 166.
10. Buchanan to Captain Engle, May 4, 1861, in Lewis, 164.
11. Buchanan to Coale, in Lewis, 166.
12. Editorial, *Mobile Tribune*, November 19, 1869, in Lewis, 254.
13. Buchanan to *Examiner*, in Lewis, 170.
14. Craig L. Symonds, *Confederate Admiral: The Life and Wars of Franklin Buchanan* (Annapolis: Naval Institute Press, 1999), 139.
15. Ibid., 227.
16. Buchanan to *Examiner*, in Lewis, 168.
17. Lewis, 159.
18. Buchanan to Coale, in Lewis, 165.
19. Buchanan, letter to the editor, *Examiner*, in Lewis, 169.

20. Symonds, 126.
21. Lewis, 252-253
22. Horace Greeley, editorial in New York *Tribune*, quoted in Lewis, 253.
23. Lewis, 253-254.

The Marylander on the Hunley

1. Bruce Smith (AP), "Hunley crewmen, RIP," *Washington Times*, April 18, 2004. A1.

Isaac Mayo Unreconstructed

1. Carl Schoettler, "Death Before DISHONOR," *Baltimore Sun*, August 11, 2003, http://articles.baltimoresun.com/2003-08-11/features/0308110212_1_mayo-revolutionary-war-arundel-county.
2. Jonathan Pitts, "Commodore Mayo: A man of adventure and tragedy," *Baltimore Sun*, May 14, 2011, http://articles.baltimoresun.com/2011-05-14_1_commodore-isaac-mayo-con.

MORE ON HISTORY

Lloyd Tilghman and the War in the West

1. James W. Raab, *Lloyd Tilghman and Francis Asbury Shoup: Two Forgotten Confederate Generals* (Murfreesboro, TN: Southern Heritage Press, 2001), 105.
2. Bryan S. Bush, *Lloyd Tilghman: Confederate General in the Western Theatre* (Morley, MO: Acclaim Press, 2006), 190.
3. Raab, 29.
4. Linda Davis Reno, *The Maryland 400 in the Battle of Long Island, 1776* (Jefferson NC and London: McFarland & Company, Inc., 2008), 3.
5. Bush, 112.

A Distant Defender of the Old Line State

1. Hester Dorsey Richardson, *Side-Lights on Maryland History,* vol. 1 (Baltimore: Williams and Wilkins Company, 1913), 406-407.

The Maryland SCV: Keeping Watch

No annotation.

CULTURE AND SOCIETY

Growing Old in the South

1. Chestnut, *Diary from Dixie,* 307.

Two Murders

No annotation.

Yankeefying Dixie

1. Clyde Haberman, "No Smoking, and Don't Try Putting It Out," *New York Times,* December 2, 2003, http://www.nytimes.com/2003/12/02/nyregion/nyc-no-smoking-and-don-t-try-putting-it-out.html.

Redneck Girls and Southern Belles

No annotation.

Beware That Which You Don't Understand

1. Bill Maxwell, "There's no place like the South," *St. Petersburg Times,* March 24, 2002.

Joyce Bennett

The Country Girl

No annotation.

On Courtesy

No annotation.

The Fall of the House of Chaptico

1. Stark Young, ed., preface to *A Southern Treasury of Life and Literature* (New York: Charles Scribner's Son's, 1937).
2. Hervey Allen, ed., introduction to *The Complete Tales and Poems of Edgar Allan Poe* (New York: The Modern Library, 1938).

Maryland in the Movies

No annotation.

Give Me That Old-Time Religion

No annotation.

The Devil Went Down to Dixie

1. Flannery O'Connor to John Hawkes, November 28, 1961, in *Letters of Flannery O'Connor, The Habit of Being*, ed. Sally Fitzgerald (New York: The Noonday Press, 1999), 455-456.

I'm OK, You're...a Yankee

1. In some parts of the South, *pecan* is not pronounced peacan, but all over the South, it is the first syllable of the word that is stressed. In the North it is the second.

Maryland, My Maryland

Saving Maryland's Southern Speech

1. Jon Ward, "Tobacco tradition terminal," *Washington Times*, March 27, 2002, A01.
2. William Eddis to "a friend,"1770, in James Breig, "Speaking with Colonial Inflections," *Colonial Williamsburg* 25, no. 3 (Autumn 2003), 83.
3. Breig, 82.
4. Robert McCrum, William Cran and Robert MacNeil, *The Story of English* (New York: Elisabeth Sifton Books, 1986), 213-216.
5. Ibid., 106.
6. Ibid., 108-109.
7. O'Connor in *Letters of Flannery O'Connor*, 566, 321, 396.
8. William Faulkner, "Spotted Horses," in Young, *Southern Treasury*, 672.
9. Margaret Mitchell, *Gone With the Wind* (New York: Avon Books, 1973), 316, 987, 138, 442, 132, 369, 357.
10. Seth Lerer, "The History of the English Language Part Two: Making Modern English," *The Great Courses on Tape* (Chantilly, VA.: The Teaching Company Limited Partnership, 1998), audio-cassette tape, 2.3.

Old Versus New Baltimore

1. Douglas, *Stonewall*, 311.
2. Fannie A. Beers, *Memories: A Record of Personal Experience and Adventure During Four Years of War* (Philadelphia: J.B. Lippincott Company, 1888; Project Gutenberg, 2005), Introductory, 6, http://www.gutenberg.org/catalog/world/readfile?fk_files=1501551&pageno=6. Citation is to online edition.
3. "200 Best of Baltimore 1997," *Baltimore Magazine*, July ? 1997.
4. H.L. Mencken, *The American Language: An Inquiry into the Development of English in the United States*, 4th ed., ed. Raven I. McDavid, Jr. (New York: Alfred A. Knopf, 1977) , 465.

5. H. L. Mencken, interview by Donald Howe Kirkley, Library of Congress, Washington, D.C., June 30, 1948, YouTube (accessed January 25, 2014). Mencken's lack of a Maryland accent is understakable given the fact that he attended, as he says in this interview, a German private school as a child. Further, Baltimore's "ethnic" communities were close knit; they were in a sense many small towns within one big town.

Halfbacks and Wannabes

No annotation.

Name of God...Yankee Ham Hocks!

No annotation.

The Southerner's Love Affair with the Tomato

No annotation.

Maryland Cookin'

1. Surratt Society, *A Taste of the Past* (Pleasanton, KS: Fundcraft Publishing, Inc., 1984), 78, 87,57.
2. Jane Bradley, *Southern Style* (Gaithersburg, MD: The American Cooking Guild, 1987), 41.
3. *The Deep South Cookbook: A Southern Living Book* (Oxmoor House, Inc., 1976), 11.
4. *The Progressive Farmer Southern Country Cookbook* (Birmingham, AL: Progressive Farmer Books, 1972), 126-127.
5. Ibid., 127.
6. Charlotte Turgeon and Frederic A. Birmingham, *The Saturday Evening Post All American Cookbook* (Indianapolis: The Curtis Publishing Company, 1976), 34, 71,145.

7. Ibid., 168.
8. Ibid., 34.
9. The Hammond-Harwood House Association, *Maryland's Way* (Annapolis: The Hammond-Harwood House Association, 1963), 330-331.

Pickin' Crabs

No annotation.

Hee Haw Redux

1. Gene Weingarten, "Below the Beltway," *Washington Post Magazine*, March 22, 2009, 28.

Maryland Is Hunt Country

1. *Maryland's Way*, 169.
2. Ibid.
3. Ibid.

GLOSSARY OF MARYLANDISMS

1. J. R. Clark-Hall, *A Concise Anglo-Saxon Dictionary* (www.bnpublishing.net: BN Publishing, 2008), 87, 84.
2. Sir William Osler, B.T., M.D., F.R.S., *The Principles and Practice of Medicine* (New York: D. Appleton & Co., 1918), 398.
3. John Neill, M.D. and Francis Gurney Smith, M.D., *An Analytical Compendium of the Various Branches of Medical Science* (Philadelphia: Blanchard & Lea, 1856), 958.

Available from Shotwell Publishing

Washington's KKK: The Union League During Southern Reconstruction by John Chodes (2016)

When the Yankees Come: Former South Carolina Slaves Remember Sherman's Invasion. Edited with Introduction by Paul C. Graham (2016)

Southerner, Take Your Stand! by John Vinson (2016)

Lies My Teacher Told Me: The True History of the War for Southern Independence by Clyde N. Wilson (2016)

Emancipation Hell: The Tragedy Wrought By Lincoln's Emancipation Proclamation by Kirkpatrick Sale (2015)

Southern Independence. Why War? - The War to Prevent Southern Independence by Dr. Charles T. Pace (2015)

For More Information, Visit us Online at
WWW.SHOTWELLPUBLISHING.COM

www.ingramcontent.com/pod-product-compliance
Lightning Source LLC
Chambersburg PA
CBHW061300110426
42742CB00012BA/1999